LIFE INSURANCE

How to Use It to Your Clients' Advantage

By the Professionals at **PartnersFinancial, an NFP Company**
Edited by **Bryan Schick, CPA**

10495-356

Notice to Readers

Life Insurance: How to Use It to Your Clients' Advantage does not represent an official position of the American Institute of Certified Public Accountants, and it is distributed with the understanding that the author and publisher are not rendering legal, accounting, or other professional services in the publication. If legal advice or other expert assistance is required, the services of a competent professional should be sought.

ISBN: 978-0-87051-897-3

Publisher: Amy M. Stainken
Senior Managing Editor: Amy E. Krasnyanskaya
Associate Developmental Editor: Allison Rudd
Project Manager: Amy Sykes
Cover Design Direction: Clay Porter

Preface

As your client's trusted adviser, you're bound sooner or later to get the question, "How do I protect my family when I die?"

Many clients think they understand how life insurance works, but in reality, most are unaware of all the potential ways it can be used. And when it comes to buying life insurance, clients especially don't understand the nuances of how it is priced, underwritten, and managed. Many clients read through the policy illustrations and see only a meaningless set of numbers. This is when they turn to you and ask, "Where are the numbers that matter, and what do they really mean?"

Life Insurance: How to Use It to Your Clients' Advantage was developed by PartnersFinancial and the AICPA to help guide you through some of the more important aspects of life insurance, with the goal of helping you better serve your clients.

As you read the pages that follow, you will learn how the life insurance industry has evolved, the key components of issuing a life insurance policy, and the tools and techniques available today.

Whether you choose to incorporate these tools by building a life insurance practice inside your firm, by purchasing or merging your practice with an existing life insurance practice, or by forming a partnership with an independent and objective insurance adviser, one thing is clear in today's environment: client demand for unbiased advice has never been higher.

Speaking as someone who has helped build many successful partnerships between CPAs and life insurance professionals, I can tell you that you are in a unique position. Clients are looking more frequently to their CPA as their most trusted adviser and asking for more and more services. For this reason, I believe that life insurance should be a part of your practice.

So, as you begin incorporating life insurance more strategically into your practice, it is the sincere wish of all of us who partnered on this book that it be an invaluable resource to you.

Peter Chung
AVP, Professional Partnerships
PartnersFinancial, an NFP Company

*   *   *

PartnersFinancial was formed 23 years ago by 5 highly successful, nationally recognized independent insurance and benefits firms in order to achieve leverage with vendors and carriers. Over the years, it has become much more—a national, close-knit collaborative network that has stimulated intellectual and financial growth of its member firms. PartnersFinancial is an organization dedicated to its members and committed to sharing knowledge with the CPA community.

Acknowledgements

This book would not have been possible without the help of many generous people at PartnersFinancial and National Financial Partners Corp. who volunteered their time and experience. We especially wish to acknowledge our members who authored the invaluable case studies in this book, and whose input and guidance have separated mere theory from what actually works in the real world.

Specifically, we thank Richard Baer, Bill Black, Jay Cavanagh, Kyle DeVries, Gregory Freeman, Nathaniel T. Harris, Stephan Hubbard, Paul Jablon, Ellwood L. Jones, Jordon R. Katz, Barton Kaufman, Robert Kelly, Mark Kosierowski, James Monteverde, Julian Movsesian, Marc Parkinson, Donald R. Payne, Ron Perilstein, Sam Radin, Kenneth Samuelson, Robert Schechter, Simon Singer, D. Gregory Steliotes, Edward L. Wallack, Mark P. Winter, Bradley Zapp, Matthew P. Andersen, John Conti, Justin Pehoski, Trish Sumpter, Amanda Zukowski, and Bryan Schick, CPA, for making financial planning appear fascinating and learnable.

We are also indebted to our leadership for their encouragement and support: R. Bruce Callahan and James R. Gelder, for their many years of valuable experience and for teaching us the real art of managing client relationships, and to John Irvin, a true professional with an unflagging commitment to quality, one who is willing to go the extra mile to make a difference.

All of us wish to publicly express our gratitude to one another for coauthoring this book and to Amy Stainken, Martin Censor, Amy Krasnyanskaya, and Andrew Grow of the AICPA (our publisher), who have provided support, encouragement, and friendship. Their patience and professionalism kept this book moving forward to a successful conclusion.

Finally, our greatest appreciation goes to all of our member firms. Without their unwavering confidence and unselfish support, we could never have undertaken this project.

To all of you, our most heartfelt thanks.

Contents

Chapter 5—Life Insurance Policy Management and Advice

Chapter 8—Life Insurance Premium Financing and Life Settlements

Chapter 9—Private Placement Life Insurance and Corporate and Bank Owned Life Insurance (COLI/BOLI)

Resources

Using the Life Insurance Training CD-ROM

To help you better understand and explain the basics of life insurance products to your clients, we have included five supplementary training modules on the CD-ROM found with this book. These self-paced, interactive Adobe® Flash® lessons will help you to:

Lesson One: Introduction to Life Insurance
- Define life insurance
- Differentiate between term and permanent life insurance
- Describe the various types of permanent life insurance
- Explain the concept of insurable interest
- Name two rating systems for life insurance companies

Lesson Two: Term Life
- Define term life insurance
- Describe the three basic types of term insurance
- Explain the renewability and conversion features
- Identify typical riders used with term insurance

Lesson Three: Whole Life
- Describe the characteristics of whole life insurance
- Name the premium payment options typically available
- Define "cash value"
- Explain the various dividend options typically available
- Describe the features of a typical policy loan provision
- Recognize some popular whole life insurance policy riders

Lesson Four: Universal Life
- Distinguish the characteristics of universal life
- Explain the flexible premium structure of universal life

- Determine how the cash value accumulates
- Describe current and guaranteed interest rates
- Name the common expenses associated with universal life
- Identify the differences between death benefit options

Lesson Five: Variable Life
- Describe the characteristics of variable life insurance
- Explain how variable life is regulated
- Identify common premium payment options
- Discuss various investment options
- Address expenses associated with variable life
- Explain how death benefit amounts are calculated

The minimum system requirements in order to run and view these lessons properly are:
- Microsoft® Windows® Operating System
- Intel® Pentium® II 450MHz, AMD Athlon® 600MHz or faster processor (or equivalent)
- 128MB of RAM
- **Note:** The Flash® presentations on this CD-ROM may not run properly on Mac computers or the Linux operating system.

How to Use this Book

Disclosures Before Case Studies

Asset Allocation

Using asset allocation as part of your investment strategy neither assures nor guarantees better performance and cannot protect against loss of principal due to changing market conditions.

Case Study

The following case studies are based on actual client situations but are meant for informational purposes only. The case studies are in no way intended to be used as a primary basis for insurance or investment decisions. Similar results are not guaranteed and will vary based on the individual client situations. Clients should consult with their own financial, tax, legal, and accounting advisers before implementing any insurance or investment plan. Neither the information presented, nor any opinion expressed, constitutes a solicitation for the purchase or sale of any security or investment product.

Tax and Legal

This material is for informational purposes only and is not meant as tax or legal advice. Please consult with your tax or legal adviser regarding your personal situation. Neither National Financial Partners Corp. nor any of the individual advisers from the case studies offer legal or tax advice.

Circular 230 Disclosure: To ensure compliance with requirements imposed by the IRS under Circular 230, *Regulations Governing the Practice of Attorneys, Certified Public Accountants, Enrolled Agents, Enrolled Actuaries, Enrolled Retirement Plan Agents, and Appraisers before the Internal Revenue Service*, we inform you that any U.S. federal tax advice contained in this communication, unless otherwise specifically stated, was not intended or written to be used, and cannot be used, for the purpose of (1) avoiding penalties under the Internal Revenue Code (IRC), or (2) promoting, marketing, or recommending to another party any matters addressed herein.

Life Settlements

Investors should consult with their own professional adviser regarding the potential tax, estate, and legal considerations that may arise in connection with entering into a life settlements transaction.

Proceeds from a life settlement transaction may be taxable under federal or state law to the extent the proceeds exceed the cost basis. The proceeds from a life settlement transaction may be subject to claims of creditors. The receipt of proceeds from a life settlement transaction may adversely affect eligibility for government benefits and entitlements. The amount received for the sale of the policy may be affected by the circumstances of the particular purchaser of the policy, the insured's life expectancy, future premiums, the death benefit, the terms of the policy, and the current market for insurance policies, among other factors. The amount received for the sale of the policy may be more or less than what others might receive for the sale of a similar policy. There may be high fees associated with the sale of a life settlement.

COLI/BOLI

Insurance products (1) are not a deposit or other obligation of or guaranteed by any bank or bank affiliate; (2) are not insured by the Federal Deposit Insurance Corporation or any other federal government agency or by any bank or bank affiliate; and (3) may be subject to investment risk, including possible loss of value.

Guarantees are subject to the claims-paying ability of the issuing insurance company.

Withdrawals made during the first 15 years could result in unfavorable last in, first out (LIFO) taxation under IRC Section 7702(f)(7) "force-out" rules. Withdrawals in excess of cost basis may be taxable. Lapsing a policy with an outstanding loan results in the loan, and any accrued interest, being treated as a distribution, which may be taxable. Modified endowment contracts (MECs) are taxed differently and are not suitable for this program if surrenders or loans are anticipated. Please check policy illustrations to see if the policies being considered are MECs. Certain changes to a non-MEC policy could result in the policy becoming an MEC. Professional tax advisers should be consulted. Any loans, withdrawals, or partial surrenders will reduce cash values and death benefits.

Mutual funds and variable life insurance policies are sold by prospectus and private placement memorandum only. The investor should consider the investment objectives, risks, charges, and expenses of the investments carefully before investing. The prospectus and memorandum contains this and other information. Please read these carefully before investing. In the event you need an updated copy, please contact your NFP Securities, Inc. representative.

Past performance cannot predict future results. The purpose of this discussion is to present the issues and plan mechanics associated with a taxable investment and corporate/bank owned life insurance. The insurance products shown in this report are representative of the market and are based on a hypothetical investment yield, which is not guaranteed.

IRC Section 7702A defines an *MEC* as a life insurance policy that has had cumulative premium payments made during the first seven years that exceed the sum of net level premiums (the seven-pay test). Net level premiums are determined by each insurance company and reflect the premiums required to "pay up" the contract during the first seven years. The carrier must assume guaranteed cost of insurance charges and guaranteed minimum interest rates for "7702" testing, which determines the net premium.

Disbursements from MEC policies, other than at death, are taxed on a LIFO basis, accessing cash value buildup first and owner's basis last. Disbursements from non-MEC policies, other than at death, are taxed on a first in, first out basis, accessing owner's basis (premiums paid) first and cash value buildup last.

Case Studies

Throughout the text, you will find case studies that demonstrate for advisers' applications of life insurance concepts in financial situations common and uncommon to affluent families and businesses.

The goals of these case studies are to

- increase your perspective of the scope of life insurance as an effective planning tool for businesses and families.
- help you to more effectively diagnose from your clients' fact patterns and thought processes potential problems and opportunities in which life insurance could have an important role.
- share the lessons learned from our successes as well as our occasional missteps.

Many nonmaterial elements of these case studies have been adjusted to preserve privacy and confidentiality of actual clients. To keep the focus conceptual, all numbers are simplified by rounding to appropriate zeros.

Please note that the information included in the case studies is for educational purposes only and not intended to solicit or sell any products or services. The names have been changed to protect the identities of the individuals involved. The information should not be applied or relied upon in any particular situation without the advice of your tax, legal, or financial services professional. The views and concepts expressed may not be suitable for every situation. This material was created to provide accurate and reliable information on the subjects covered. It is not intended to provide specific legal, tax, or other professional advice. The services of an appropriate professional should be sought regarding your individual situation.

Investments are not guaranteed and are subject to investment risk including the possible loss of principal. The investment return and principal value of the security will fluctuate so that when redeemed, may be worth more or less than the original investment. Generally, the greater an investment's possible reward over time, the greater its level of price volatility or risk.

(Using diversification and asset allocation as part of your investment strategy neither assures nor guarantees better performance and cannot protect against loss in declining markets.)

(Variable annuities are long-term insurance contracts designed for investing for retirement. An annuity offers options under an insurance contract, which includes mortality and expense risk charges as well as providing for lifetime payments. They offer the opportunity to allocate premiums among fixed and variable investment options that have the potential to grow income tax-deferred, with an option to receive a stream of income at a later date. Early withdrawals may be subject to a deferred sales charge and, if taken prior to age 59½, a 10 percent federal penalty may apply. Money distributed from an annuity will be taxed as ordinary income in the year the money is received.)

Opinion Disclosure

The opinions expressed in this book are those of the author and may not necessarily reflect those held by National Financial Partners Corp. (NFP). The material is for informational purposes only. It represents an assessment of the market environment at a specific point in time and is not intended to be a forecast of future events or a guarantee of future results. It is not guaranteed by NFP for accuracy, does not purport to be complete, and is not intended to be used as a primary basis for investment decisions. It also should not be construed as advice meeting the particular investment needs of any investor. Neither the information presented nor any opinion expressed constitutes a solicitation for the purchase or sale of any security.

Introduction

Why do you need this book?

For virtually all of your clients, their first life insurance purchase was a risk management decision.

All insurance starts with risk management. Most kinds of insurance mitigate the financial impact of *possible* adverse events. *Life* insurance stands apart because it protects against only one event that is not just a possibility but an inevitability: death. The risk is that it will occur at a time that will undermine the financial security of the surviving family members or business partners or any other parties who will be affected.

Your clients' life insurance decisions provided them the confidence that financial security could be maintained, family lifestyle would continue, and business success would not be interrupted. They trusted that the family or business would have the resources to make a fresh start, and felt assured that planned expenses for the future could be met.

Once those life insurance decisions have been made, most clients put their policies into their files and ignore them. What more is there to do? Maybe, as their success grows, they will ask their advisers to evaluate their coverage in light of their current financial resources and determine whether or not they are *underinsured*.

That's one kind of vigilance professional advisers should perform; but for the affluent families and successful businesses that make up your client base, it remains a fraction of what you can and must do for them.

If risk management were the only reason to buy life insurance, obviously there would be very little to write about in this book. However, your clients need to make life insurance decisions, and advisers need a higher standard of life insurance knowledge.

Life insurance decisions today are capital management decisions.

The capital management role of life insurance transcends the relatively uncomplicated world of risk management to a higher—and much more complex—plane of family and business success. Now you have to integrate family and business capital with tax law and tax strategy in relation to immediate, intermediate, future, and even multigenerational goals. You need to develop client plans that incorporate intricate legal structures and detailed documentation to grow, protect, and preserve capital. Most important, the plan has to effectively address your clients' values—deeply-rooted hopes and fears, aspirations and goals, beliefs, and philosophies.

How is that possible when life insurance capital remains an unknown concept for policyholders and encompasses a planning area generally underdeveloped by their advisers? To answer that, you need to ask the right questions about life insurance.

What makes life insurance capital different?

In mid-2004, President Bush proposed a vision of America as an *owner-ship society*, explaining, ". . . if you own something, you have a vital stake in the future of our country. The more ownership there is in America, the more vitality there is in America, and the more people have a vital stake in the future of this country."

The idea had been blossoming for over a decade. But how many Americans immediately thought about the life insurance policies they owned? How many suddenly realized that owning life insurance made them an integral part of the ownership society?

Remember the television commercials from many years ago, in which a camera tracks through a party of stuffy moneybags putting on airs about their investments? Then the only normal-looking guest is asked what his broker recommends, and he starts to say, "My broker is E.F. Hutton . . . ." Now the room goes utterly silent as everyone strains to hear what E.F. Hutton recommends.

Do you think there has ever been a party conversation that starts with, "What life insurance do you own?"

It wouldn't halt the party for a moment, it would end it.

But between the E.F. Hutton commercial and President Bush's vision of an ownership society, something changed the financial landscape and transformed life insurance. In the 1980s and 1990s, the number of Americans who became capitalists by taking ownership of public companies skyrocketed. Consider the following:

- Stocks and bonds and real estate began to move from the Monopoly board into the lives of the middle class and wage earners.
- Mutual funds offered the potential security of diversification and eliminated the anxieties of picking stocks.
- Homeowners began viewing their house not as their family home but as their largest family investment.
- 401(k) plans forced employees to take a more active role in long-term financial success.
- Subscriptions to the *Wall Street Journal* mushroomed, and financial planning books and magazines took over whole sections in bookstores.
- Personal accountants expanded their client relationships beyond tax season to become year-round advisory resources.

In that same period, life insurance underwent a series of product transformations that made its capital management capabilities more apparent—without sacrificing its traditional risk management role. And the effectiveness of that dual role, compared to other strategies for creating and protecting wealth, has three components unique to life insurance:

- *Life insurance tax structure.* Capital inside a life insurance policy grows income tax deferred, and multigenerational capital in the form of the death benefit is received income tax-free—and estate tax free with the right ownership structure.
- *Life insurance cost structure.* Life insurance cost is determined primarily by mortality costs plus marketing and administration overhead, so increases in longevity along with more efficient systems lowers costs for consumers.
- *Life insurance flexibility.* Policyholders have choices for the capital invested inside their policies between increased performance control or increased protection guarantees.

Integrating these components effectively depends on personal and business philosophies, capital management goals and objectives, and financial and tax circumstances. No different from the decision process any investment requires.

But because sophisticated advisers and consumers continue to look at life insurance from the narrow perspective of risk management, they miss capital management opportunities. Without the advanced knowledge that life insurance capital management requires, they fail to consider life insurance strategies with the same care they give to investment strategies.

Even language gets in the way. Consider the following:

- You *make* investments, but you *buy* life insurance.
- You can call yourself an *investor*, but you can't call yourself an *insurer*.
- Investments make you a *capitalist*, but life insurance vernacular implies you are simply a *consumer*.
- You can talk about your latest investment at a party and sound cool, but talk about your latest life insurance policy and you are suddenly alone in a corner.

How do policyholders and their advisers lose control of life insurance capital?

It's easy to know how the stocks you own are performing. You have nonstop access to virtually any investment in any market through multiple online sources. You can track your investment strategies and make decisions accordingly. Everybody can—at any moment.

How would you find out if your life insurance policies are underperforming? It's not that easy. Where would you go online? Life insurance companies generally do not support online access to policies.

The life insurance companies from whom you purchased your policies send a policy statement once a year or quarterly for some kinds of policies. The statement's content provides only a snapshot with nothing to compare the information.

You could ask the companies for an in force illustration—assuming you reached the right voice mailbox and knew the right words to use (newer policies are required to send an in force analysis). Then you would have to wait for paper copies to be sent to you.

But after the wait, what would an in force illustration tell you? It would tell you the present value of your policy with projections going forward based on current assumptions.

If you could actually find and interpret that information in the spreadsheet formats with line after line of disclaimers, you could compare it to the illustration you received when you purchased the policy to see if you were ahead or behind the original projections.

If you own a variable life insurance policy, some companies allow online access to the investment subaccounts, but not to the policy itself. So you can see how the funds in the subaccounts are performing, but you typically cannot view the values in your policies online.

Why are life insurance companies so far behind the curve compared to other financial services providers? Part of the reluctance to provide online services is the risk of fraud. If an insurer pays out a claim to the wrong individual, they have to pay the same amount to the right individual and may never recover the mistake.

For that reason, not only can you not access your policy for performance evaluation, you can't even change your address or make any other material changes without using paper and ink. It is their traditional form of protection, and they are comfortable that way. Besides, consumers are not asking for more.

And that is, by far, the more important reason—the continuing acceptance of life insurance as a buy-and-hold contract. It's generally true that life insurance policies are built to last for decades. But your clients' circumstances don't stay the same for decades, not even for years or, in some cases, months. Yet they have millions and tens of millions of dollars (family and business capital) tied up in life insurance policies.

In fact, life insurance companies are full of good people, and they can lay claim to strong guiding values and high fiduciary standards. They privately acknowledge the need for policy management and accept, in theory, that evaluating policy performance is the responsibility of prudent policyholders—a right they exercise over the personal capital they have *invested* in their policies.

In general, they are not pushing any envelopes' edges to develop the tools for that responsibility, simply because they see no corresponding edges in the marketplace. But one or two have made investments in developing policy management tools for policyholders that trigger action items, help evaluate policy performance, and help decision-making. If these tools prove valuable to policyholders and their advisers, the rest of the industry will automatically follow their lead.

Let's hope it is not too little, too late. The changes that have taken place since the 1980s in the financial world, generally, and in the insurance industry, specifically, have intensified that responsibility. Not only should policies be subjected to more diligent and timely evaluation because of these changes, but the number of options for poorly performing policies has multiplied.

In many cases, there will be no reason to make a change. The policy may be performing adequately or even dramatically well. And isn't that something your clients know?

Maybe a policy is performing less than brilliantly—meaning, for example, that the projected paid-up premiums are actually not paid up because the policy cash value has not earned enough to meet the premiums without an infusion of outside cash. Your clients definitely want to know that—and well in advance to avoid a very big surprise.

As a professional adviser for clients with large amounts of capital in life insurance policies, you have to ask yourself the following questions even if your clients accept the responsibility for life insurance capital management, and even if your clients can access the information somehow from the life insurance companies

- are they really capable of making informed capital management decisions?
- do they see the big picture and the implications of their options?
- can they find the details they need in the numbers?
- will they be able to integrate their life insurance capital management decisions with other components of their financial and tax planning?

No. You need to help them.

What do advisers need to know to help their clients?

Life insurance is a complex financial product. How it is constructed can be very difficult to understand. Many of us with long personal histories in the life insurance field are frequently surprised to come across life insurance agents who seem to struggle to understand it.

This volume is designed to enable professional advisers to counsel clients from the perspective of an educated and well-informed understanding of life insurance policies and their operation over time. We will deconstruct life insurance to its basic components, rebuild them in the many forms that life insurance takes today, and then apply life insurance solutions to specific problems your clients will encounter and opportunities your clients should know about.

It seems that the easiest way for people who have deeper specialized knowledge in some field to confuse the rest of us—pick anything tied to the digital world we inhabit, for example—is to create an impenetrable jargon full of phrases stolen from other contexts, made-up words, and annoying acronyms. You will see examples of the life insurance versions of these as you read ahead, but we will make every effort to explain them.

You will also see case studies throughout the following text that illustrate diverse applications of life insurance that fit many of your clients. It is beyond the scope of your professional practice to duplicate solving these problems and capturing the opportunities, but it is integral to your practice to see the potential they offer your clients.

Your clients' knowledge stops somewhere in these three bullets. You can get them past the blockage:

- They appreciate the value of protection against adverse financial impact of death, but they may not know enough to make informed decisions to achieve that goal effectively.
- They may doubt that their current life insurance is still financially viable, but they may not know how to make comparisons.
- They don't know what they don't know about life insurance and will miss opportunities to use it as a more effective financial tool to resolve a range of financial issues.

Professional advisers need to take a proactive role in life insurance knowledge to assure their clients make informed decisions. It has become part of your professional standards and your professional liability. This book is designed to help fill the gap.

Life Insurance Policy Evolution and Structure

1

The Evolution of Life Insurance Policies
Term Life Insurance Policies

The simplest form of term insurance is available for a period or a term of one year. Generally, all life insurance policies are based on the risk element associated with this type of life insurance, commonly known as *yearly renewable term* insurance, or, in industry jargon, YRT.

YRT premiums are based on the projected number of deaths among the insured population of the same age and class.

With respect to age, the operative principle is that as the population ages, more deaths occur. So a YRT product has an annually increasing premium that reflects the increased risk of death.

With respect to class, such products recognize the difference between men and women and their respective mortality rates by placing them in certain categories or risk classifications. A standard risk is the base risk classification, and an insured can be better or worse. For example, a *preferred risk* means lower mortality, a lower chance of death in the coverage year, and lower premiums. A *rated* or *substandard risk* means a higher mortality, a higher chance of death in the year of coverage, and higher premiums. The impact of using tobacco products on mortality is significant enough to have a separate classification.

YRT policies are generally perceived as the lowest cost insurance, but as the risk of death increases, so do premiums. What happens as the cost of coverage rises over time?

Long ago, insurers found most insured individuals declined to continue their coverage after a number of years because the premiums became too expensive. This was particularly true among individuals whose policies were more than 10 years old. Such voluntary terminations of coverage before death were and are profitable to insurers; however, this meant that consumers were not prepared for the adverse financial impact of death.

The term insurance product design did not meet the need for affordable policies that could be maintained until death. Whole life policies were invented in an effort to fill this gap.

Whole Life Insurance Policies

A whole life policy charges a higher but constant annual premium for the life of the contract. The premium is determined at the age of the insured when the policy is issued. For example, a 40-year-old male would pay the same premium each year until the policy matures. A 41-year-old male would pay a higher annual premium to reflect his older age, but such premium would be constant until the policy matures.

What makes such level premiums possible in a whole life policy is the policy's guarantee that the policy's cash value will be equal to the insurance amount (that is, death benefit) when the policy matures (typically at age 100). For example, a $1 million whole life policy will endow (that is, $1 million of cash value) at age 100 if premiums are paid each year.

Such cash value builds up gradually over the life of the insured individual. As it does, the amount of pure risk insurance diminishes, and the individual self-insures to the extent of the policy's cash value. The difference between the cash value and the insurance amount is known as the *net amount at risk* (NAR or NAAR).

If a $1 million policy that was 10 years old had $100,000 of cash value, the NAR would be $900,000—$1 million minus $100,000. As in the case of the YRT product, a higher unit charge exists for the $900,000 of insurance to reflect the fact that the individual is now 10 years older and part of a group with more deaths annually than the group of individuals when the policy was issued 10 years earlier.

A whole life policy has three guarantees:

- Guaranteed amount of insurance—death protection
- Guaranteed amount of required annual premium
- Guaranteed amount of cash value as scheduled on a yearly basis

A whole life policy can be described as a nonparticipating or a participating policy. A nonparticipating policy is typically issued by insurers that are stock companies owned by their shareholders. A participating policy, the most common type, is issued by mutual insurance companies that are owned by their policyholders.

Mutual insurers pay their policyholders' dividends because policyholders participate in the dividends declared by the company, hence, a participating policy. Insurance policy dividends represent a return of excess premiums and generally are based on the insurer's savings in any or all of the three following areas:

- Lower mortality costs than projected mortality (fewer deaths than expected)
- Higher interest earnings than the guaranteed interest earnings, for example, 6 percent realized over 3 percent guaranteed
- Expense savings realized in the operation of the company compared to the projected expenses.

Many agents believe that in the early years of a whole life participating policy, mortality and expense savings might represent about 25 percent of the source of dividends, and interest earnings might represent 50 percent. They also believe that in the later years, after approximately 20 years, the interest earnings might represent about 75 percent of the source of dividends, and the remaining 25 percent would be attributable to mortality and expense savings together.

The savings are referred to as a *return of excess premiums* because, in effect, the insurer has overcharged the policyholder and has returned such overcharge as a dividend representing excess premiums.

Whole life policy dividends play an important role in the cost of such a policy. They are *not* guaranteed and properly should be viewed as highly variable. Dividends can be used to purchase paid-up additional insurance, to reduce premiums, to purchase term insurance to cover the amount of a policy loan secured by the policy cash value, or can be received as cash.

An additional dividend option that is rarely used is known as "dividends on deposit." With this option, dividends earn interest; however, the interest is subject to current income tax.

Dividends are most commonly used to purchase paid-up additional insurance. These can also be used to make a policy self-sustaining after paying premiums for a number of years. The term *self-sustaining* should be understood to mean that the payment of premiums in cash from the policyholder's funds will not be required. From this point on, premiums are paid by using dividends and the policy's accumulated cash value rather than from a cash payment. Additional cash payments may be required if the dividends and guaranteed cash value are not sufficient to maintain the policy in force.

Whole life policies did meet the need for coverage that could be maintained until death but were generally perceived as expensive, particularly in comparison to term insurance. In order to provide a lower cost form of permanent insurance, a new product was invented: universal life insurance.

Universal Life Insurance Policies

The Internal Revenue Code (IRC) uses the term *flexible premium adjustable life insurance* as the formal name of universal life (UL) policies.

In the simplest of terms, universal life is a combination of term insurance and an interest-bearing cash value account that resembles a money market fund.

The insurer credits the fund with a current rate of interest that it declares. Such interest rates can be changed frequently, for example, monthly, and mirror changes of interest rates in the credit markets. Typically, the insurer invests in debt instruments with a duration that matches that of the liability (approximately averaging to a duration of 5–10 years), subtracts a spread to cover their expenses, and earns a small profit. The net amount is the interest rate credited to the universal life policy. An insurer can either use a new money or portfolio approach to crediting interest. A new money approach will track market conditions more rapidly, whereas a portfolio approach blends the new investment returns with the older in force investments to determine the rate. A whole life policy follows a portfolio approach.

Because the interest earned is inside a life insurance policy, it is not subject to current income taxation. To the extent that such interest earnings are used to offset the policy's current charges, the cost of insurance is being paid with pretax rather than after-tax funds.

Universal life insurance differs from whole life insurance most dramatically in the flexibility of premium schedules. Premiums can be level, front-loaded, skipped, reduced, or increased, as may be appropriate. For this reason, universal life is not a static product and must be monitored annually.

Universal life products could not have achieved popularity without computers because each policy must be designed before purchase. For example, one could design a universal life policy to require a premium in all years that would cause the policy to endow at age 100, or one could design the same policy to have one dollar of cash value at age 100.

Many policyholders and their agents tend to not monitor their universal life policies, a practice that has led to many unhappy policyholders whose policies lapse due to the lack of additional unplanned premiums. In order to address this issue, insurers developed new UL products with secondary guarantees.

Secondary guarantees provide that if a premium payment schedule selected by the policyholder is followed and it equals or exceeds the secondary guaranteed premium for that same payment period, the policy will not lapse, and the scheduled premium amounts will not be increased.

Although such policies have become very popular, the guarantees lead to low or no cash value so that the policies look like a form of permanent term insurance. For this reason, some clients prefer "current assumption" universal life policies because these accumulate cash value that may be used for other purposes. In addition, pricing, premium flexibility, and cost recovery at surrender are other reasons why some clients prefer current assumption universal life policies.

UL generally met the demands of most life insurance clients: affordable coverage and a policy that could be maintained until death. However, as time passed, clients and agents became more sophisticated and saw the potential of life insurance as an investment vehicle. Based on this vision, a new type of product was created, variable universal life (VUL).

Variable Universal Life Policies

The universal life policies previously described are also known as *fixed* universal life policies. This "title" distinguishes them from variable universal life insurance policies.

VUL policies are essentially the same as fixed UL policies, but instead of cash value that is credited with interest at a rate declared by the insurer, the policies have many different subaccounts from which the policyholder may select. The subaccounts offer different investment choices managed either by the insurer or outside managers. The funds include index funds, equity funds, bond funds, and international funds.

One of the advantages of a variable insurance policy is that the policy values are held in a separate account of the insurance company rather than its general account; therefore, the funds are not subject to the claims of the insurer's creditors. In this respect, the separate account is not dissimilar to funds held by a bank in its capacity as a trustee.

A VUL policy is more complex and, therefore, has higher internal expenses than a UL policy. Such expenses include not only the mortality and expense charges of a UL policy but also charges that are levied on the assets under management in each subaccount.

Further, the managers of the subaccounts levy a similar charge at the fund level. The rationale for a VUL policy is that over the long term, it will be less expensive than a UL policy because the policy's equity returns should be higher than the returns of a UL policy because, generally speaking, stocks outperform bonds.

Because of the availability of such investment choices and because the policy values can grow in a tax deferred environment, VUL policies are often used as accumulation policies rather than death benefit policies. For a VUL policy to be effective as an accumulation vehicle, the death benefit (insurance amount) must be as small as possible while still meeting the IRC's definition of a life insurance contract.

A VUL policy is a registered security. As such, a greater need is to make sure that the policy is a suitable product for the purchaser. If the policyholder cannot sustain the risks of principal loss or higher premium demands caused by reduced investment returns, the policy is not suitable and should not be recommended.

One other attractive feature of a VUL product is the ability to make it into a synthetic UL policy by investing in the insurer's fixed account, which is generally backed by the same type of bond portfolio that supports a UL policy. In addition, when the fixed account is selected, the expenses associated with fund management usually do not apply.

VUL policies are complex financial instruments. Like UL policies, they must be monitored regularly to prevent policy degradation. Many policyholders with large VUL policies review performance reports as frequently as quarterly or monthly.

Because VUL policies tend to be riskier than traditional UL policies but typically offer better returns, insurance companies saw the need to create a product that could still be considered a good investment vehicle and offered clients some type of "protection" against the markets ups and downs. From this idea, indexed universal life was created.

Indexed Universal Life Policies

Indexed universal life (IUL) is the most recent addition to the panoply of insurance products. Such policies are similar to traditional UL policies but have a different way of crediting interest. IULs link the investment return of the policy to the performance of certain financial indexes such as the S&P 500, the Dow, and the Hang Seng, to name a few.

IUL differs from UL and VUL in several ways. First, unlike VUL, currently IUL is not considered to be a security; therefore, this product is not regulated by the Securities and Exchange Commission (SEC), and the agent does not need to be securities-licensed to sell the product. Second, the returns are hedged to reduce or limit the investment risk. Third, a guaranteed minimum threshold of performance and a cap on positive performance exist.

IULs have a fixed rate component with a minimum guaranteed interest rate, as well as a choice of indexed account options. Policy owners can direct their premiums into the fixed account or into the available indexed accounts, or both. IULs guarantee a small annual return through allocations into the fixed account and have the potential for an additional return based on the linked indexes' performance.

When premium is directed into any one of the indexed accounts, an indexed account segment is created. The index growth is calculated at the end of the segment or period. The most common index crediting method is annual point-to-point. With this method, the beginning index value is compared to the ending index value at the end of the period (one year), and if the ending value is higher, the interest is credited to the policy. If the ending value is not higher, no interest is credited. A few other common index crediting methods are five-year point-to point, monthly averaging, and daily averaging. The different methods offer different performance structures.

The interest credited to the policy is subject to the participation rate or growth cap, or both. The *participation rate* is the percentage of positive movement that is credited to the policy during the segment. For example, if the S&P 500 increased 5 percent and the current annual participation rate is set at 80 percent, the policy would be credited 4 percent at the end of the segment. The *growth cap* is the maximum interest rate that will be credited to the policy for the segment. Typically, insurers offer a minimum participation rate or growth cap, or both. It is important to note that participation and growth cap rates can be changed at any time at the insurer's discretion.

The policy is also subject to the floor rate, which protects the policy from negative returns in down years. The *floor rate* is the minimum interest rate that will be credited to the policy for the segment. Typically the floor rate is set at around 0 percent.

IUL policies temper the risk and reward element of a VUL policy. In theory, such policies have lower operating costs than a VUL, yet are intended to produce returns that exceed those of a UL policy because the underlying indexes are expected to outperform the typical mid-term bond portfolio that supports UL investment returns (declared interest rates).

The various internal policy charges for mortality expense and operating expense and the offsetting credits for positive investment performance operate in essentially the same manner as in a UL or VUL product.

Life insurance, regardless of the policy type, has evolved into an asset that is unique among financial instruments. It is a long-term product and, therefore, must be monitored and managed to achieve the best results and lowest cost. To monitor and manage effectively, advisers need to understand the structure of each type.

Life Insurance Policy Structure

In 1984, the Deficit Reduction Act (DRA) clarified for the first time what life insurance is for tax purposes. It describes life insurance in terms of requiring an amount at risk. The act states "only the excess of the amount paid by reason of the insured's death over the contract's net surrender value shall be deemed to be . . . life insurance . . . ."

The effect of these few words is to create a tangible, quantifiable structure for life insurance in terms of whose capital is involved. The net amount at risk is the money in the contract that does *not* belong to the policyholder. It is life insurance company capital, which, in the event of the insured's death, is paid to the policyholder. At death, this insurance company capital is transformed into beneficiary capital, income tax free.

What does the insurance company charge for this net amount at risk? Like any manufacturer, it must pay the business expenses associated with the design, production, marketing, and servicing of the product. But uniquely, life insurance is a promise to pay a specified amount to beneficiaries at the time of the insured's death.

And for that it must also assess mortality charges, the cost calculated for meeting this obligation. Other factors aside, because increasing age increases the chances of dying, mortality costs increase each year of a contract and are expressed as a cost per $1,000 of life insurance.

From this perspective, it would seem that life insurance can be reduced to the factors mentioned in the DRA definition. All life insurance contains these costs, no matter what kind of policy is used to structure the promise to pay. Does that mean your clients no longer need to be confused by all the different types of insurance?

Unfortunately, not. Although there may be one factor common to all types of insurance (one understood in terms of the net amount at risk and its associated cost), the real differences of life insurance policies and the source of much of the confusion for your clients come down to the most efficient way to pay these costs.

Payment Structure

With term insurance, no surrender value exists because the net amount at risk is the only capital in the policy. Premiums are paid by the policyholder to meet the expense and profit projections of the insurance company. Insurance companies determine by actuarial science and underwriting procedures how much to charge to cover expenses and death benefits occurring before the term ends, given that they will not have to pay anything to policyholders who outlive the term.

This is pure risk management for as long as he is alive during the term of the contract. The death benefit represents future capital to be managed for beneficiaries in case the insured does not.

So the policyholder must reassess the immediate financial risks he is managing with the policy and the future capital management impact of the death benefit for heirs in light of the higher cost of term insurance at renewal. He or she may decide to lower the coverage or pay higher premiums for the new term coverage or convert the policy to a cash accumulation policy for life.

Cash accumulation policies, developed to create a permanent life-long policy without a break in insurance between the old term and new term, offer a different way to pay. Policyholders invest funds in excess of what is required for the cost of insurance, letting the insurance company invest their money to build earnings inside the policy on an income tax deferred basis.

Cash accumulation policies also add a current capital management dimension for the policyholder on top of the risk management element.

Because your clients now have their own money in the policy in excess of the cost of the protection offered by the policy, you have to step beyond the most efficient way to pay and determine the most effective capital management using the tax structure of life insurance. In effect, what you pay for is not what it costs.

Death Benefit Structure

With a policy covering one individual, death benefits are paid to beneficiaries immediately upon proof of death. However, when the risk of financial loss is tied to the second of two people dying, a survivorship policy is often more appropriate.

Survivorship policies, also known as *second-to-die*, are life insurance policies that cover the lives of two people, most commonly a husband and wife. The death benefit is paid only after the death of the second insured.

Pricing advantages are gained with the survivorship policy structure compared to the same total coverage under two single life policies. Underwriting tends to be more liberal in some cases, allowing an insured who may have been denied coverage for health reasons under a single life structure to be approved for coverage by a survivorship product. However, someone who is denied coverage under an individual policy will pay a higher cost of insurance as an uninsurable rate class under a survivorship policy.

Tax Structure

For all forms of life insurance, the death benefit is paid to beneficiaries income tax free.

The reason for this advantageous end result is rooted in the use of tax law to shape social policy. In terms of the number of policies in existence, an overwhelming majority are purchased purely for the financial protection of family members against the untimely death of an income-producing family member, or, in the corporate world, to the financial security of a business against the untimely death of an owner or key employee.

Supporting the financial security of families and businesses is good social policy, so life insurance death benefits remain tax-free. The fact that this tax advantage can significantly benefit other obviously tax-based applications of life insurance has not changed the death benefit tax protection.

In addition to the income tax free death proceeds for beneficiaries, with cash value policies, the cash accumulation component grows tax-deferred as long as the policy is maintained. One impact of this tax-deferred growth is that some of the cash accumulating in the policy represents prepaid premiums and, therefore, some of the cost of insurance will be paid with cash accumulating tax-deferred inside the policy, or, pretax money.

If the policy is surrendered before death, income tax has to be paid on the growth of the cash value over the client's basis in the contract or premiums paid. So whether the policy is kept or surrendered, the tax structure of cash accumulation policies favorably affects the cost.

Partial surrenders are possible in whole life policies in which additional money is invested in the policy in the form of paid-up additions. These function as component policies within the policy with cash accumulation and death benefits self-contained as a paid-up addition. Surrendering the paid-up addition does not affect the structure of the policy but only removes that component's death benefit and cash values underlying it.

Partial surrenders are also available in universal life policies as a policyholder takes back cash value, which reduces death benefit amounts correspondingly.

Policy loans are a potential capital management tool for policy-holders. They may borrow up to the amount of the accumulated cash value through one or more loans. Interest is charged on a policy loan and will be charged for as long as the loan is unpaid. If the annual loan interest is not paid when due, the loan itself will increase annually by the amount of the unpaid interest, which is commonly referred to as *capitalizing the interest*. If the policyholder dies while a loan is outstanding, the amount of the loan, plus any unpaid interest, will be deducted from the death benefit, with the beneficiary receiving the remaining or *net* death benefit.

As long as the policy remains in force, policy loans are not taxable income. However, if the policy loan is still outstanding when the policyholder surrenders the policy, or it lapses, the amount of the loan, including interest due, will be considered taxable income to the extent that there is gain in the policy.

Modified Endowment Contract

Typical of all areas of financial services in the 1980s, innovative ways to push the envelope in the investment world led to what the government considered abuse of life insurance tax advantages. Consumers were pre-paying large policies as a way to shelter capital inside the tax benefits of life insurance.

To correct the perceived abuse, Congress limited the amount and rate at which money could be put into a life insurance contract without tax consequences. When those limits are exceeded, the life insurance contract is considered a modified endowment contract (MEC) from that time forward.

During the first seven years of the contract, premiums are limited to the net level premiums that would be needed if paid on a level basis to purchase a paid-up policy at the end of seven years, an amount determined by the insurance company that is commonly referred to as the *seven-pay* or *MEC premium*. And if premium payments are higher than the cumulative amount of level premium needed during any of those first seven years, the policy is considered an MEC for tax purposes. Insurance companies generally will let policyholders know if they get a premium that will create an MEC and give the policyholder the option of simply getting that money back instead of having it applied as premium.

Once a life insurance policy becomes an MEC, all policy distributions—surrenders, partial surrenders, and loans—are then taxable as ordinary income to the extent cash surrender value exceeds the investment in the policy. In other words, first in, first out is changed to last in, first out. Plus a 10 percent penalty will be imposed, with certain exceptions based on age, disability, and payment structure.

Policies that are materially modified after the seven-year period must be retested, as must survivorship policies in which the face amount is reduced after seven years.

However, despite the change in tax treatment for money coming out of the MEC during the contract holder's lifetime, death benefits from an MEC remain income tax free.

Because most policies are monitored to avoid being classified as an MEC, there may be a tendency to consider MECs as somehow "illegal" life insurance policies. But there can be situations where an MEC is suitable for the financial and tax goals of the contract holder because the financial advantages are not affected by the potential tax consequences.

Life Insurance Pricing

2

Introduction to Pricing

How would you price a completely intangible product? It is a promise to pay an agreed upon amount at some time in the future if and when a specific event occurs, which in this case, is death. By definition, the ultimate value of the product will be realized only when the insured is no longer available to judge.

So although the variables are initially mathematical, financial, and medical, that is, reasonably scientific and dependable, the actual cost of the product cannot be quantified until the contract is completed. Meanwhile, the ability to meet the contractual obligation depends on the manufacturer's success in measuring risk, investing money, and controlling costs over potentially decades of the policyholder's life.

Impossible? It will sound *less* impossible if we start with the simplest pricing structure—term insurance.

Pricing Pure Term Insurance

Term insurance is simpler because no investment component exists—no distinction between insurance company money and policyholder money. All the policyholder money in the policy is used to cover cost and profit, and no policyholder money is in the contract that is not money at risk.

For term insurance, pricing starts with the probability of death occurring during the term of the policy. To that the manufacturer adds the expenses in bringing the product to the market and servicing it over the term of the policy. Then it must estimate the yield it can achieve by investing that money, while allowing for the profit goal. Finally, pricing is determined from the state of the policyholder's health. If he or she passes a physical exam, the policy can be issued.

One other pricing component exists that is discussed in a different context in the following text. Not all term contracts are held until death generally because increasing premiums become too expensive in the later years of the policy. When a policy lapses, the insurer can save a substantial amount of money, so lapses can affect product pricing and insurer profitability.

If the earnings are sufficient to pay death benefits and cost and achieve the profit goals, everyone wins.

Pricing Term Insurance With an Upgrade

Many prospective term policyholders would prefer to have an option of continuing coverage beyond the term without going through the same process. Life insurance companies offer term insurance that is guaranteed renewable and convertible; in other words, coverage can be continued for another term or converted to a permanent policy without additional underwriting.

This gives the policyholder more control of the coverage and forces the manufacturer to assume more risk. Price goes up accordingly to cover the risk, but still the money in the policy remains insurance company money. And both kinds of policies—pure term and guaranteed renewable and convertible term—are purchased with after-tax dollars.

Pricing Life Insurance With Policyholder Capital Added

Except for one element, the pricing factors for the insurance company remain in place when policyholder capital is invested in life insurance policies. Policyholder capital grows tax-deferred, and the gains can be used to pay for the cost of coverage on a pretax basis. That element is one factor that brought whole life insurance products into the marketplace.

In whole life policies, the insurance company money at risk remains the term insurance component of the policy. The policyholder pays more premium than needed for the cost of pure term, and the money is credited with interest and dividends based on the company's ability to grow the money.

Premiums remain constant for the entire contract, which can be until the policyholder's death or endowment, and so does the death benefit. Therefore, the manufacturer must price the product to account for variations in mortality, expenses, lapses, and investment results over a very long period.

Meanwhile the policyholder must pay the premiums. If the policyholder fails to pay the premiums, the life insurance company can extend the coverage for whatever period the cash value in the policy will fund. Or, the policyholder can take the cash back at the cash surrender value—the cash value minus costs recovered by the insurer.

Premiums have to be paid every year, but some flexibility exists about where those payments come from. Dividends from the policy can be applied to premium. Paid up additions can be purchased that can later be applied to premiums, and policyholders can borrow from the cash value to pay premiums.

Because those limited options for paying premiums, in many cases, did not make financial sense for policyholders, the advice to "buy term and invest the rest" gave the investment world a chance to capture investor money that would otherwise go into whole life policies.

Life insurance companies responded with universal life, a new policy structure that increased flexibility.

Pricing With Flexibility Added

Interest-sensitive whole life, universal life, variable life, and variable universal life originated as hybrids of whole life in which control of the basic components shifts between insurance company and policyholder.

With universal life, the insurance company has control over investments, but increases policyholder control of premium payments. Cash value becomes a reservoir to pay premiums and support the death benefit.

As with a whole life insurance policy, universal life policy (UL) premium payments go into the insurance company's general account. The general account invests to earn revenue that goes back to the policy as interest. If the policyholder does not want to pay the premium for any period, the insurance company will pay itself out of cash values, with a possible impact on the amount of death benefit that the policy can support.

The trade-off for this premium flexibility is that death benefit is no longer guaranteed by the insurance company—only by the premiums paid and the growth performance of the cash component of the policy.

Because policies are purchased based on projected values that may or may not be realized, policyholders have to manage the values in their UL policies more carefully.

But the obstacle to managing the values in their policies is the fact that the life insurance company controls the crediting rate and the cost of insurance factors in the cash value growth. The next evolution offered a new level of flexibility for policyholders: control over the investment component of their policies that came with the development of variable universal life (VUL).

VUL shifts control of all three elements—investment choice, premium payments, and death benefit—to the policyholder. Increased control increases the opportunity to accumulate higher cash value than nonvariable products but at the same time increases the risks by removing traditional guarantees for rates of return and death benefits.

VUL policies add a new concept for consumers to understand: separate accounts. Premiums do not go into the general account of insurance company. Instead they are put into a separate account designated for the policyholder. The policyholder then manages the investment allocation of that account.

Separate accounts have a wide range of investment choices and asset allocation strategies. As the performance of markets varies up and down (thus, the term *variable*), policyholder separate account values vary up and down, building cash value in line with the account gains. Loans of cash value are also affected by the variable nature of VUL, and loan amounts are generally limited to 70 percent to 80 percent of cash value.

Pricing With Added Guarantees

With all this new-found flexibility and corresponding performance risk now in the hands of policyholders, many found over time that they could not manage their policies effectively enough to maintain the death benefit without having to pay additional premiums out of pocket. UL policies offer two crediting rates—current and guaranteed. When rates of return decline generally, even the guaranteed rates may be too low to maintain the cash value needed to pay premiums.

Because many policyholders tend to forget that the growth of cash values were simply projections based on a set of assumptions that were reasonable at the time the policy was purchased, the reality check of cash values not meeting projections came as a shock and upset financial planning efforts for many.

So policyholders started asking for guarantees, and many of their accountants and other advisers began recommending guaranteed products to protect them from underperforming cash values and increasing mortality charges.

But the problem of eating cake and having cake always comes up when consumers flip back and forth between mutually exclusive alternatives. Insurance companies could add guarantees back into the picture, but there would have to be a trade-off.

Here is how it is done. Parallel to the guaranteed policies that policyholders purchase is a "shadow" account maintained by the insurer in its computers that functions like the current account value in the universal life policy structure. In this virtual account, the crediting rate and cost of insurance assumptions are managed by the insurer and tend to be more favorable than the guaranteed and current assumptions shown on the illustration. The shadow account performance determines how long the guarantee will go out. Typically, there is minimal to no cash value in the actual policy, which is, in some way, a trade-off for the guarantees.

It's no surprise a trade-off exists for guarantees in any financial product. In addition, an additional cost exists for a rider that adds a guarantee to the insurance policy.

Pricing With Increased Unpredictability

Actuarial, underwriting, investing, and management skills combine to make pricing of insurance products effective. With all this expertise at work, the intangible nature of the product does not make it unmanageable as long as all other factors remain reasonably predictable.

One recent unpredicted change that has been of tremendous benefit to consumers is the substantial increase in life expectancy brought about by advances in medical science and practices. Consumers deserve credit as well for making better individual health and lifestyle choices.

The result has been the updating of actuarial information and lowering costs for life insurance coverage. Only a few years of added longevity can have significant impact on life insurance pricing. The change is most apparent in the simplest form of protection, which is term life insurance. Over the last decade, the cost of term insurance has dropped significantly. This is primarily due to the fact that people are living longer. However, lower term insurance costs have also pushed term insurance costs lower still.

Say that again? Lapse rates, as previously described, can have a big impact on policy pricing. As term rates have fallen because of longer life expectancy, policyholders in larger numbers have replaced existing term coverage at a lower annual premium, even though the insured was older. Carriers respond by repricing term rates based on a higher lapse rate resulting in lower term rates and higher lapse rates.

Because term policies are relatively easy to understand and compare, a large share of the marketing of term life has shifted from agents to the Internet, reducing costs as well.

Also, the illnesses that were fatal to the last generation are now chronic in this generation and may be eliminated in the next. This trend will continue as long as medical science finds ways to keep us alive longer. Life insurance companies have responded by extending coverage. Permanent policies that, until recently, provided coverage to age 100 are now being written to age 120.

But the negative impact of unpredictability was demonstrated dramatically much earlier. In the 1980s and 1990s, the life insurance environment underwent complex changes. The financial services industry began erasing distinctions between disciplines and expanding choices for consumers. The result was competition that pushed companies to take pricing steps for current marketing reasons that were, no doubt, difficult to justify based on traditional pricing wisdom.

During the same period, a truly global economic environment emerged that made long range forecasting highly unreliable. New technologies and applications were developing in such rapid cycles that tremendous promise could turn flat just as quickly.

In previous decades, the life insurance industry had enjoyed steady, gradual increases in interest rates and decreases in mortality. Actual policy performance usually exceeded anticipated performance. Premiums were constant. Product pricing was under control, so much so that costs could be quoted from a rate book.

When financial markets were finally hit by change, interest rates declined and a 30-year trend came to an end. Dividends and other nonguaranteed pricing factors had to decline correspondingly. The bulk of policies in force in the early 1980s no longer performed as illustrated.

The reasons involve factors both within and completely outside the control of the companies issuing the policies. But lowered performance resulted in unanticipated premium increases or dividend reductions, jeopardizing policy benefits and the goals and planning strategies to which they were linked.

For consumers and their advisers, the "price" of a policy was, at one time, quoted from a rate book. But the personal computer replaced the rate book with a product illustration. The contrast was obvious because the illustration ran for pages of spreadsheets that were incomprehensible to consumers.

Worse, clients, advisers, and even some agents tended to confuse an illustration of policy values with the contractual provisions of the product, so that an illustration which demonstrated attractive values became synonymous with a "good" insurance product.

In this era, the most common illustration demonstrated the "vanish" premium concept. This type of illustration showed the death benefit and cash value continuing after the out-of-pocket premiums stopped ("vanished" was the buzzword), and was based on assumptions not guarantees. When markets took their inevitable downturn, premiums not only did not vanish, in some cases, they had to be increased to prevent policy lapses.

Not surprisingly, clients and advisers felt betrayed as they saw the amount of annual premiums or number of years to pay increase and learned that the original premium schedule, perceived as a sure thing, turned out to be only an estimate. In addition to the negative impact on policy performance, the revised premium schedule disrupted gifting plans and split dollar arrangements. Many policies suffered from the additional constraint of large surrender charges, which prevented clients from receiving all of the cash value if they surrendered the policy. This contract feature eliminated the possibility of exchanging the policy for a better performing product.

The policy illustration was the document that should have communicated the value of the product in clear terms that allowed consumers to understand what they were buying and how they were paying for it so they could make comparisons and arrive at informed decisions.

Here are the actuarial pricing components that become assumptions driving illustrations in permanent policies. They are not particularly complex by nature, but it is easy to see how the application of these components can bend product pricing beyond the consumer's ability to judge value.

Interest Crediting Rates

One thing that makes interest rates difficult to interpret and compare is that they do not always reflect the same information. The rate credited to the accumulation component of a policy can be a gross rate before any expenses are subtracted, a net rate including investment expenses, or a net rate including investment expenses, as well as other expenses and profit loads.

Interest is credited as dividends and excess interest credits in participating policies. These are considered a return of excess premium for tax purposes, reflecting the fact that the company earned higher returns or experienced lower expenses and passed some of the gain to its mutual policyholders. Dividend interest rates are usually net of interest expense. Nonparticipating policies and other product types may use interest rates net of both investment and company expenses and profit loads.

One more component is needed in determining what the rates actually mean—the method of calculating the crediting rate. Beyond the rates shown in the illustration used at the time of purchase, when it comes to actually crediting the interest rate for policies in force, two distinct methods of interest allocation exist—*portfolio* and *new money*.

The portfolio method determines the total investment return on the portfolio of assets held by the company. All polices are credited at the same interest rate, whether they were purchased years before in previous interest environments or purchased in today's interest environment. This results in more stable rates of return over time, but one group of policyholders effectively subsidizes another, depending on the interest environment at the time of purchase.

The new money, or investment year, method separates each calendar year block of policies, tracking the assets and investment income related to each block. That is arguably more equitable from an individual policyholder point of view, but subjects the crediting rates to more visible fluctuations as the markets go up and down.

For a policy remaining in force over a long time period, an equalizing effect takes place, which eliminates the differences between the two approaches. So the method is not critical to policy performance as much as it is critical to initial comparison of one policy to another. If different allocation methods are used, depending on the current interest environment, one policy may illustrate considerably better, though ultimately, the advantage may be illusory.

The understanding of interest rates should help an adviser to judge how policy results may change as crediting rates vary over time. If the current rate is not supported by current experience or is supported by a portfolio rate that is different from current new-money rates, then a future change should be expected even in the absence of a change in new-money market rates.

Of course, if pricing is not supported by current experience, then clients are, in effect, assuming the risk that future performance will not meet pricing requirements. From the clients' perspective, the critical concern is not so much how the policy itself may change, but what the changes might mean to their planning objectives.

Related to crediting rates, for example, one planning objective might be to achieve cash flow advantages by utilizing the policy's cash value growth for premium payments. If it is important for a premium to remain "vanished," then the policy should be funded initially based on a more conservative interest rate.

Interest rate remains the pricing factor with the largest impact on the policy performance. This impact is greatest on high cash value products. As cash value decreases, the effect of interest variation decreases, and the effect of mortality variations increases.

Mortality

Companies compare their actual claims experience to the assumption they used in pricing the products. This is called an "actual to expected ratio." One hundred percent indicates that actual claims are equal to priced-for claims; 110 percent means that the company has worse mortality experience than is priced for in their products; 90 percent mortality ratio says that fewer insureds died than expected. Companies track their actual to expected ratio over a number of years and should they see a definitive trend of actual to pricing, the mortality assumption used in pricing new products will change. Sometimes the favorable or unfavorable mortality experience is passed along to in force policies as well.

Expenses

In the same manner as the mortality ratio, the company expense ratio can be expressed as actual expense levels divided by priced-for expense levels. A resulting percentage below 100 percent indicates the pricing has that much tolerance for unanticipated expenses. Beyond that tolerance is the area where, if it continues for a period of time, pricing on new products can increase.

Lapses

Using the same method, the lapse ratio compares actual lapse rates to priced-for lapse rates. If lapse support is a pricing factor, and lapses do not occur as priced-for, then the original illustrated results may not be achieved, and price adjustments will have to be made.

Taxes

Both state and federal taxes are part of life insurance pricing structure.

At the federal level, insurers are taxed in effect on deferred acquisition charges. These are costs that are incurred in the year the policy is issued, and insurers amortize the deduction. To replace cash flow lost as a result of deferring deductions, companies add a charge to premium that is called the deferred acquisition cost, or DAC tax.

States tax insurers a premium tax on all premiums paid to the insurer—varying among states from 1 percent to around 3.5 percent. This can offer a price advantage particularly for insurance owned by irrevocable life insurance trusts, in which a lower state premium tax could be achieved by meeting the guidelines set by insurers about state residence for grantors, trustees, and trust instruments.

So—What Is the Lowest Cost Life Insurance?

Unfortunately, this question has survived far beyond its usefulness. It made sense only in a financial environment in which life insurance was seen as a necessity for the protection of spouses and children should the breadwinner die and in which only two product choices existed—term and whole life—and from company to company, there was little distinction.

In such an environment, it can make perfect sense to ask for the cheapest product. But the question, and the environment supporting it, belong in the Smithsonian today. Life insurance is now recognized as a capital asset requiring a management approach like any other capital asset.

For consumers who only need and want basic protection against the financial impact of dying during a period of their lives, term insurance resolves the issue. Pure term insurance can be bought in a commodity-like manner over the Internet, given adequate information about the financial condition of the company issuing the policy. But a large and growing segment of consumers needs more from life insurance. They need the right product to integrate with complex and long-lasting planning goals.

This segment represents more affluent individuals, particularly business owners and highly compensated corporate executives and professionals, as well as the firms they own and manage. They would not make "cheapest" the only criterion for purchasing anything else in their personal or business lives, but well-meaning financial columnists and professional advisers still tell them to buy the cheapest term—ignoring everything else they have written or said about sophisticated financial planning.

And even more surprising, they recommend submitting specifications to several agents to assure low cost. The flaw in this bidding approach is that rather than utilizing their design expertise and resources, the bidding agents are forced into a cheapest policy response, which may not be in the clients' best interest.

Another flaw in this process arises from the manner in which the insurance industry shares data on work in progress through an independent information bureau. When several agents are working on the same case, the same insurer may see the case several times and will understand that it is being submitted to other companies as well. In this scenario, agents who have a demonstrated track record of quality business with carriers may lose their ability to achieve favorable contract conditions for their clients. The carrier's hands are tied by the fact that multiple agents have submitted the same case and cannot use subjective criteria.

In working with their affluent clients, whose needs may be very specialized and sophisticated, buying decisions driven by a simplistic *lowest cost* goal are likely to go awry. These kinds of clients need to understand that low cost can equate to low value in a way that undermines the plan altogether.

Advisers and clients alike need to recognize the role of a knowledgeable and responsible life insurance professional with considerable experience in the subtleties of family and business decision-making, who can walk them through the complexities of life insurance products and their applications.

But there is no substitute for consumer knowledge. The pricing factors in life insurance contracts are part of that. They are put to the test with the product illustration, and much has occurred in the past decade to make illustrations clear and reliable.

Life Insurance Illustrations 3

In the 1980s and 1990s, a wave of new product development rolled through the industry. Until then insurance products were largely commodities, and marketing distinction was based more on the company brand—stability, safety, size, and so forth. The change challenged insurance companies to gain marketing edges through product features.

Because the personal computer had taken over the way product features were communicated to consumers, computer-generated product illustrations became the most important point of sale tool. And creativity went over the top—creativity in actuarial analysis, in underwriting policy, and in agent "tweaking"—until product illustrations became tools to tailor life insurance products to specific individual needs.

Because illustrations are just calculations based on a set of assumptions, consumers were forced to make decisions after staring blankly at pages of spreadsheets that covered decades of their lives. Getting a second opinion from another agent didn't help; it made the confusion twice as bad. Illustrations could dramatically produce more favorable results over decades simply by modifying one assumption that clients had no way to interpret. Everybody was talking about apples and oranges, but it was more like cherimoyas and carambolas.

What was lost in all the exercises in flexibility was the fact that the illustration *is not* the product. No matter what results could be projected to meet client needs, the product wasn't guaranteed to perform that way. And if it did not, then the client needs very likely would not be met.

When three straight decades of market growth stalled out in the 1990s, policyholder expectations were not being met, and their planning decisions began to unravel unless additional cash could be injected into their policies. Because they were under the impression that the illustration *is* the product, agents and companies came under fire.

Clearly, the illustration as a decision-making tool was the heart of the problem. If consumers could not see the assumptions or understand the numbers that the assumptions created and could not detect which elements of the policies were guaranteed and which were not, then, at best, policy illustrations were worthless and, at worst, deceptive. The industry had to respond immediately.

New Illustration and Market Conduct Standards

To make illustrations reliable for consumers and advisers, the National Association of Insurance Commissioners (NAIC) created the Life Insurance Illustrations Model Regulation, which sets the standards for presenting life insurance product data for informed decision-making in order to put the value of life insurance products on a level playing field.

A second organization has added parallel oversight to curb illustration abuses and make it easier for clients to analyze and compare life insurance products. The American Council of Life Insurance (ACLI) formed the Insurance Marketplace Standards Association (IMSA), a self-regulatory organization, to promote the ACLI's Principals of Ethical Market Conduct.

In addition, because variable life insurance products place investment risk in the hands of the policyholder, they straddle insurance and securities and fall under regulatory control of both the Securities and Exchange Commission and state insurance commissioners. Agents authorized to sell variable life insurance must be licensed by the state and by the Financial Industry Regulatory Authority (FINRA) as registered representatives of a broker-dealer and are subject to FINRA rules for full disclosure with compliance maintained by the broker-dealer. Securities law related to investments also covers variable products.

These efforts are in response to a life insurance sales process that came to rely far too heavily on illustrations demonstrating product performance. If one company illustrated more favorable projections, another company need only tweak the assumptions to go one better. But the math was only as good as the assumptions, and more complicated math did not improve the assumptions.

For example, some companies assumed that their operating expenses would fall as reorganization plans took effect. Other companies assumed that a significant number of those who purchased a policy would surrender it before it matured as a death benefit claim.

Advisers—let alone their clients—could not always tell which illustrations were based on credible assumptions. Their fallback was to rely on the technical expertise of the insurance agent selling the policy. Unfortunately, agents usually did not have access to the actuarial assumptions underlying the product and often lacked the resources to thoroughly evaluate what they were selling.

NAIC Requirements

The NAIC Regulation addresses these issues with a two-part approach that stiffens actuarial requirements for the nonguaranteed values shown in insurance illustrations and also mandates that specific information be shown to any prospect. Insurance companies are required to follow the regulation when conducting business in those states which have adopted it (39 as of December 2009), but many companies have been voluntarily complying in all states since the regulation was established.

The Companies' Responsibilities

To comply with the first part of the NAIC Regulation, the insurance company must annually certify to the state insurance commissioner that each set of assumptions used in calculating the illustration, such as interest rates, expense charges, or mortality costs, is based on the actual recent experience of the company. The company must also certify that it will break even on the product at or before the 15th year, which reduces the likelihood that it will increase charges to policyholders in order to remain profitable. Finally, the company must certify that it will break even at or before the 15th year even if everyone who buys a policy keeps it. This last requirement is intended to prevent companies from simply assuming that they will not have to pay death benefit claims for a large number of policyholders.

The reliability of these certifications is open to question. Some critics of the industry contend that these tests limit only the worst abuses because of gaping loopholes. First, the myriad factors involved in the interpretation and actual application of the two tests create opportunities for aggressive actuaries to obfuscate unrealistic assumptions. Second, a product can honestly pass the break even test and still fail to meet the profitability goals set for it by the company. Finally, the tests must be passed only in the aggregate for all ages of insureds, so insurance companies can still favor particular ages with aggressive assumptions. More likely sales scenarios, such as paying annual premiums for 10 years, can also be favored, with these assumptions offset at other ages or scenarios.

The Agents' Responsibilities

The term *agent* means representative of the manufacturers—not a salesperson, but someone who can act as their official spokesperson and can interpret their information in the interests of the client. The regulation reinforces this role by establishing standards responsive to the interests of the client.

Agents presenting these illustrations must comply with the second major part of the regulation by giving the client a basic illustration, which includes the narrative summary, the tabular detail, and the numeric summary. The basic illustration must be page numbered, (1 of 12, 2 of 12, and so forth) assuring that the client receives all the pages.

It must be signed by the client, acknowledging,

> I have received a copy of this life insurance policy illustration and understand that any nonguaranteed elements are subject to change and could be either higher or lower. My agent has told me they are not guaranteed.

The narrative summary contains a description of the type of life insurance policy and definitions of key policy terms. Many of these key terms have their origin in life insurance marketing as branding strategies, but including their definitions gives them legitimacy and gives advisers and clients a more reliable understanding of the benefits provided by the policy.

The tabular detail must show the premium outlay and mode (annual, quarterly, monthly) that the client intends to pay and the guaranteed death benefit and the guaranteed cash surrender value that will result from those premiums.

Nonguaranteed values that have been certified under the first part of the regulation can be included in the tabular detail. They must be clearly identified as nonguaranteed and must be preceded by the guaranteed values. The tabular detail of some illustrations show the guaranteed values on an entirely separate page, whereas others include a set of columns for guaranteed and nonguaranteed on the same page. In either case, care should be exercised in selecting the appropriate set of figures when evaluating an illustration.

Agents are allowed to show the nonguaranteed values on a supplemental illustration to increase readability and comprehension or to demonstrate specific formats. And because of its relative simplicity, the supplemental illustration could be made the focal point of the insurance sales presentation. But it must be accompanied by a basic illustration and must refer to that illustration.

The third element of the basic illustration is the numeric summary, which includes the client signature line. It shows policy values for years 5, 10, 20, and, if applicable, age 70 based on the anticipated premium outlay and three scenarios—the guaranteed values, the nonguaranteed values, and the midpoint values.

The midpoint values are those produced using policy charges and crediting rates, which are the average of the illustrated and the guaranteed rates, that is, half-way between the two rates. For example, if the illustrated cost of insurance (COI) charge is \$2.35 per thousand, and the guaranteed COI charge is \$9.47, the midpoint values would be based on a COI charge of \$5.91. For participating policies, which rely on dividends rather than crediting rates, the dividends are reduced by 50 percent. For each of these scenarios, the summary must include the premium outlay, the policy cash and surrender values, and the death benefit. Each scenario must also disclose when the policy would lapse if that occurs before maturity or age 100.

The use of midpoint values is intended to provide the client with a range of performance expectations. Most insurance companies do not expect to ever charge or credit the guaranteed rates in their cash value policies, but it is just as unrealistic to assume that none of the charges or credits will ever deviate from the current rates. The midpoint values provide a glimpse of the performance of the contract under reduced assumptions, but they should not be the only look at reduced scenarios. Accountants should advise their clients to request complete illustrations based on crediting rates of 100 or 150 basis points below the current rate when evaluating coverage. These reduced rate illustrations should demonstrate the additional years of funding required to achieve the original policy goals or show performance based on the original premium schedule.

It is equally important to temper any evaluation of midpoint values with a review of the insurance company's financial condition and, if possible, the degree of conservatism built into the company's actuarial testing process. A company in a strong financial position, or one using more conservative assumptions, may be less likely to move towards the midpoint values than a company experiencing financial difficulty. The major ratings agencies give an indication of the company's position. Publications such as the American Society of Chartered Life Underwriters and Chartered Life Financial Consultants Illustration Questionnaire, or more in depth policy-specific analysis, may be necessary to evaluate the level of conservatism in underlying assumptions.

Ongoing Responsibilities

The regulation also addresses the question of the need for continuing client communication after the policy has been issued. Insurance companies are required to provide annual reports to any policyholder who was issued a policy covered by the regulation. The annual reports must show the policy cash value as of the last annual report and as of the end of the current period, as well as the surrender value and death benefit as of the end of the current period.

An in force illustration is not required, but the report must advise the policyholder that an in force illustration is available and recommend that the policyholder request one before considering replacing or changing the contract. The use of in force illustrations has become more prevalent in the industry. The insurance company is required to provide a prominently displayed notice of any adverse change in the nonguaranteed elements of the policy.

The policyholder must also be advised if the current cash value, plus any scheduled premiums, will not support the policy to the next reporting period based on guaranteed values. However, if policyholders are using the annual reports properly by comparing the actual values to the projected values shown on the basic illustration, they will be aware of any impending policy lapse long before this notice appears.

IMSA Requirements

If the NAIC Regulation is a "micro" approach to reform, the IMSA requirements are the "macro" equivalent. The goal of this self-regulatory organization is to establish membership in the association as an insurance industry *Good Housekeeping Seal of Approval*.

The standards are codified in six sweeping principles to which no one could seemingly object, including a 1990s version of the "Golden Rule" that states that companies will treat others the way they would like to be treated. The principles commit the member companies to ideals such as "competent and customer-focused sales and service," "active and fair competition," and producing "sales materials that are clear as to purpose, and honest and fair as to content." The member companies also agree to maintain a system in oversight and review "designed to achieve" these standards.

As with any broad ethical statement, specific situations can be troublesome in defining exactly what activities will comply with the standard. These definitions are important because evaluators from the IMSA will be examining company practices and awarding the membership designation. The variety of marketing channels used by different insurance companies can mean that what is reasonable for one company is unreasonable for another. The IMSA faces the challenge of developing guidelines that are stringent enough to be meaningful, yet broad enough to encompass a diverse industry.

Understanding What Illustrations Illustrate

In order to distinguish clearly between projected and guaranteed values, guaranteed values are presented as the worst case scenario for the product's performance.

In a traditional whole life policy, that means projecting values based on dividends of zero so that projected growth of cash value shows only the guaranteed increases contractually required to support the death benefit.

Universal life policies project guaranteed values using the guaranteed interest crediting rate and guaranteed maximum charges.

Variable life policies have no guaranteed cash values. The worst case scenario is projected using zero return on investments. However, zero is not actually a guarantee because negative returns are possible depending on the policyholder's fund selections. Some of the newer variable life policies offer shortened death benefit guarantees (that is, 5–35 years) or riders that can guarantee the policy for the life of the insured, or both.

Insurers must use current values in their projections. For whole life policies, this means applying current dividends to the projection. For universal life policies, this means applying the current interest rate and mortality charges. Variable life values depend on the policyholder fund selection, so projected rates are hypothetical and cannot exceed 12 percent. A historical look back would infer that a "safe" projection rate would range from 6 percent to 8 percent.

An illustration typically shows four components that demonstrate projected performance over time—net outlay (premiums paid minus policy distributions), account value, surrender value (the account value less the surrender charges), and death benefit. These components can be used to assess policy performance on an apples-to-apples basis.

Net present value calculations using a common interest rate provide a way to compare several policy designs on an equal basis. The information tells the prospective policyholder how much it costs in today's dollars to maintain the same death benefit using different payment strategies or different policies.

The internal rate of return on cash value calculation tells the prospective policyholder what annual return would have to be achieved if premium payments were invested in a side fund to have an equal value to the cash value amount in the policy in any given year.

The internal rate of return on the death benefit shows the annual return that the cumulative premium payments would have to earn to equal the death benefit in a given year.

Questioning the Illustration

What are the right questions to ask to protect and manage capital inside of a life insurance policy? The following are some detailed questions to clarify pricing issues in illustrations that can have a significant impact for your clients.

Term Policy Illustrations

- What is the premium and payment mode?
- What does the designated risk class mean? Are there better risk class categories?
- Are ages determined on an *age nearest* or *age last birthday* basis?
- How long is the illustrated level premium paying period?
- How long are the level premium rates guaranteed?
- How long is the policy renewable? What are the terms?
- Can this policy be converted to a permanent contract? What are the terms and conditions?
- Do waivers of premium benefits continue beyond the term of the policy?
- Are the current rates illustrated based on required reunderwriting at some future point?

Permanent Policy Illustrations in General

- What is the premium and payment mode?
- What does the designated risk class mean? Are there better categories available? What are the guidelines to obtain various risk classes?
- Are ages determined on an *age nearest* or *age last birthday* basis? Is backdating available?
- Is the death benefit level increasing or return of premium?
- Are any optional benefits included (features and riders) that are available at no additional charge?
- What riders (optional features for which there is an additional charge) are available?
- Are death benefits illustrated on an *end-of-year* or *beginning-of-year* basis?
- What methods are available to access policy cash values without surrendering the policy?

(continued)

(continued)

- If you take loans from the contract, is the interest rate fixed or variable?
- What is the effect on the death benefit if cash is withdrawn from the policy?
- Are the illustrated gross premiums guaranteed? If so, for how long?
- What is the premium that must be paid so that the guarantees stay in force to the desired age and year?
- For guaranteed contracts, what is the grace period in case premiums are not sent in on time?
- What is the guaranteed interest rate?
- What is the current interest rate?
- Is the current rate a gross or net rate?
- Do the illustrated cash values represent actual surrender values?
- How long is the surrender charge period?
- When can the policy face amount be decreased or increased? What are the terms?
- By when do the 1035 exchange monies need to be received by the company so that they can be treated as if received on the issue date? Or will a new illustration have to be provided when the 1035 monies come in?
- If the interest rate drops by 1 percent or 2 percent on a suspended premium illustration, what is the effect on the number of years that premiums must be paid?
- Is the total death benefit provided through a base policy, or is a term rider (that is, supplemental coverage) used for a portion of the coverage? (With term riders, the annual outlay is reduced, but the level of guarantee is also reduced, and the sensitivity to changes in dividends or other nonguaranteed elements is often increased.)
- If the term rider is removed, how does that affect other benefits and policy features?
- If the policy is guaranteed, is the supplemental coverage also guaranteed for the same length of time? If not, how long is it guaranteed?

- If an increasing death benefit has been chosen, how long is the death benefit guaranteed?
- What is the difference between the rate charged and the rate credited on borrowed portions of the cash value?
- Is this a modified endowment contract?
- Does the product offer any discounts through banded rates?
- Is the mortality assumption underlying the illustration based on current experience, or does it include projected improvement?
- What services are provided after issue (by carrier or producer, or both) to provide reprojections of in force policies or to administer the pattern of planned premium payment structure, withdrawals, and loans illustrated?
- How long after a policy lapses can it be reinstated? Does the client have to show evidence of insurability for the policy to be reinstated?
- Does the company use a new money or portfolio rate philosophy?
- If rates of return, internal rates of return, or results are shown to life expectancy, what mortality tables were used in determining life expectancy?

Whole Life Policies

- If the interest rate drops after premium payments are paid from earnings, what options are available—resume premium payments, decrease death benefits, shorter period of coverage?
- Who will monitor the policy values to provide early warning that additional premiums are needed while the increasing premium amount is still manageable?
- What has been the gross interest rate underlying the dividend scale for the past five years? (Traditional participating whole life)

(continued)

(continued)

- What have been the current interest rates over the past five years? (Interest-sensitive whole life)
- Is this a participating or nonparticipating whole life contract?
- How are the paid-up additions applied (reduce future premiums or increase cash value)?

Survivorship Whole Life Policy Illustrations

- Does the insurance company offer a policy split option (for example, divorce)?
- If the insurance company allows the policy to be split into two single life policies, does the company require evidence of insurability at the time of the split?
- Does the insurance company charge for the policy split option? If so, what is the charge?
- How is the joint age calculated?
- What happens, if anything, at the first death of an insured?

Universal Life Policy Illustrations

- What is the necessary minimum premium?
- For how many years is the minimum premium necessary?
- After the minimum premium period, what triggers a policy lapse?
- Does the illustration reflect bonuses with respect to the crediting of interest? Are the bonuses guaranteed?
- What are the current cost of insurance charges per $1,000?

Survivorship Universal Life Policy Illustrations

- Does the illustration reflect bonuses with respect to the crediting of interest? Are the bonuses guaranteed?
- What is the current cost of insurance charges per $1,000 of net amount at risk?
- Does the insurance company offer a policy split option (for example, divorce)?
- If the insurance company allows the policy to be split into two single life policies, does the company require evidence of insurability at the time of the split?
- Does the insurance company charge for the policy split option? If so, what is the charge?
- How is joint age calculated?

Variable (Individual and Second-to-Die) Universal Life Policy Illustrations

- What investment funds are available?
- What are the premium loads, subaccount expenses, and policy fees?
- Does the policy have mortality and expense risk charges? Describe current and guaranteed amounts?
- Does the policy have a fixed interest account? Describe current and minimum rates. Are there any restrictions on transferring into or out of the fixed account?
- Does the policy have a guaranteed interest account? Describe current and minimum rates.
- Does the policy have any policy enhancement bonuses that are credited to the cash values?
- What has been the past performance of the investment fund?
- What is the spread between gross and net yields, and what portion is guaranteed?
- What total return is assumed in the illustration?
- Is there a guaranteed minimum death benefit that applies regardless of fund performance?
- What is the current cost of insurance charges per $1,000?

Second-to-Die Variable Universal Life Policy Illustrations

- How is the joint age calculated?
- Does the insurance company offer a policy split option (for example, divorce)?
- If the insurance company allows the policy to be split into two single life policies, does the company require evidence of insurability at the time of the split?
- Does the insurance company charge for the policy split option? If so, what is the charge?

Life Insurance Underwriting 4

The Fundamentals of Individual Life Underwriting

As a CPA, you may coordinate your client's needs analysis with an attorney, banker, or other financial adviser. When life insurance is a need for your client, whether for personal or business purposes, you can minimize common sources of discord by knowing why information is needed and what type of documentation will best support the underwriter in proper assessment of the risk.

The purpose of this chapter is to describe the underwriting process, risk assessment, ratings, and financial underwriting and provide an overview of common medical impairments and how they affect the cost of insurance. It is imperative that the risk assessment is appropriate so that the insured lives can reasonably be expected to produce the mortality objectives set by the life insurance carriers and assure financial resources for future claims and benefits payments. It is equally critical that the individual applying for life insurance receive the best possible underwriting classification—fair and equitable based on an accurate assessment of both their medical and nonmedical risks.

Underwriting

Underwriting is the process of evaluating medical and nonmedical information about an individual and determining the statistical effect these factors have on life expectancy or mortality. The underwriter must employ sound judgment based on his or her years of experience and education to read beyond the basic facts to get a true picture of the applicant's lifestyle. The underwriter's primary function is to protect the insurance company insofar as possible against antiselection. *Antiselection* is a situation in which the insured is more likely to suffer a loss than the uninsured, which leads to a lack of profitability because the premiums will not be sufficient to cover the claims. If during the underwriting process an underwriter discovers lack of candor it raises a red flag and creates suspicion that can be difficult to overcome.

The risk selection process encompasses evaluation of multiple sources of information and resources, which allow the underwriter to determine how an individual will be classified. After the classification process is completed, the policy is rated in terms of the premium the applicant will be charged. The cost of life insurance protection is based on a number of factors used by the actuary in pricing the product. These underwriting factors include age, sex, smoker status, health history, family history, face amount, motor vehicle record, and avocational activities (for example, flying, mountain climbing, motorcycle racing).

Classifying Risk

Once these factors are reviewed for their plusses and minuses, the insured is assigned to an underwriting risk category. Most carriers now have three to seven risk categories. For the purpose of this discussion, they will be grouped into general categories of preferred (above average life expectancy), standard (normal life expectancy), substandard Class (lower than normal life expectancy), and uninsurable Class (greater risk than the insurance company is willing to assume).

Preferred Class

Individuals who don't use tobacco, don't participate in extreme sports, have excellent family history, ideal height and weight, and excellent blood pressure and cholesterol levels will, in most cases, fit into the Preferred Class.

Standard Class

This class is reserved for individuals who have measurements that are outside of the preferred class but have a normal life expectancy based on their risk factors. In the standard classifications, you will find greater leeway on the family history, height and weight, and blood and cholesterol levels. In some cases, individuals with a history of early stage cancer with excellent follow-up may qualify for the standard class.

Substandard Class

Individuals placed in this class have medical or nonmedical factors that make their life expectancy lower than normal. A person in the substandard class has a higher than average probability of dying earlier than their life expectancy. Because the degree of risk is greater than average, higher premium rates will be charged.

Uninsurable Class

Individuals included in this class by an insurance carrier are considered to have a very short life expectancy, generally in the 6-month to 2-year range. Individuals seen in this class will only be considered for a survivorship policy in which two people are insured, with a death benefit that is payable upon the death of the second life.

Risk Assessment and Ratings

The cost of life insurance protection is based on a number of factors used by the actuary in pricing the product. The underwriter collects and reviews the prospective insured's personal information for these factors in order to obtain a clear picture of risk. In addition to the hundreds of medical conditions that can affect underwriting, the following are additional actuarial factors that will affect the underwriter's decision:

Age

Life expectancies decline as the issue age advances, for example a 45-year-old male nonsmoker seen as a standard risk has an average life expectancy of 34.4 years compared to 30.1 years for a 50-year-old with the same health and medical factors. Increasing age is a risk factor for overall disease, disability, and death. Age is the most important risk factor for coronary artery disease, which is the leading cause of death in the United States.

Sex

Women typically live longer than men, and death rates are higher in men compared with women in almost all countries.

Smoker status

Actuarial data prove that cigarette smokers die at a younger age, so their mortality charges are higher; cigar and pipe smokers are treated differently depending on the insurance carrier.

Family history

Insurers routinely seek information regarding family history because it has long been recognized as an important factor in identifying an individual's susceptibility to disease including cancer, heart disease, and the risk of stroke during his or her lifetime.

Face amount

People have an unlimited insurable interest in their own life; as a practical matter, carriers and their reinsurers do have aggregate upper limits, which cap out at around $150 million on an individual life or second-to-die basis.

Motor vehicle record

Speeding tickets and drunk driving arrests could foreshadow an early demise.

Avocation

Sky diving, hang gliding, mountain climbing, scuba diving, auto or motorcycle racing, and private flying can increase the risk of an early death.

General Reputation and Personal Character

Some individual's behavior may be risky and can result in negative consequences. For example, an individual with a criminal history will be cautiously underwritten. Each case is given individual consideration, and only the best case scenarios are considered.

Common Medical Disorders Found in Underwriting

In this section, we will discuss some of the most common medical disorders that are seen by the underwriter. The five impairments that have been selected are conditions that affect the general public as well as the insurance population. The consequences of these impairments can range from having very minimal affect on the underwriting classification to an uninsurable risk that cannot be priced due to the severity of the condition and its bearing on life expectancy.

Build

There is no question that additional weight leads to health problems. *Build* is the relationship of height to weight; abnormal build is one of the leading causes of substandard classifications in underwriting. Build is one of the basic life risk characteristics and one of the oldest. Increased mortality is at both extremes, for those who are obese as well as those who are underweight. Although an underweight condition may be normal, it can also be a sign of an eating disorder or an illness. Although a small percentage of obese people can be healthy, obesity predisposes individuals to coronary artery disease, diabetes, stroke, hypertension, high cholesterol, arthritis, and certain cancers including colon and prostate cancer in men, and breast cancer in women, as well as sleep apnea (pauses in breathing while sleeping).

For life insurance purposes, rates for build are based on mortality studies and the average weights found in the insured populations. Generally speaking, obesity is less of an issue in the older ages. Ratings for build can usually be reconsidered for a rate reduction if the applicant is able to sustain a weight loss or weight gain over a period of time.

Hypertension

Hypertension is also referred to as *high blood pressure* or HTN and is a medical condition in which blood pressure is chronically elevated. In most cases, the cause of the hypertension is unknown. In a small percentage of the cases the cause is known, and it is related to kidney disease, tumors, or obesity. Blood pressure can be worsened by alcohol (over 3 drinks a day), stress, smoking, or high salt intake. Most people affected by high blood pressure have no symptoms, and the insurance exam may be the first time this condition is identified. Factors affecting blood pressure include lack of exercise, tobacco products, being overweight, and age. An increased risk of hypertension exists in men and postmenopausal women. Whether hypertension is treated or untreated, the level of blood pressure elevation and the presence of other cardiovascular risks like diabetes, elevated cholesterol, and smoking will determine if an additional rating will be required.

Blood pressure that is chronically elevated is a risk factor for strokes, heart attacks, and heart failure. Hypertension is the leading cause of chronic renal failure and is linked to death in insulin-dependent diabetes. Apart from age, the level of blood pressure is the most powerful single predictor of future mortality. Even mild hypertension significantly shortens life expectancy.

Blood pressure measurements typically are included as part of defined preferred criteria. Individuals who are scheduled for an insurance exam should be advised to avoid caffeine, smoking, and alcohol 24 hours prior to their exam because these substances can significantly elevate blood pressure.

Coronary Artery Disease

Coronary artery disease (CAD) is most commonly due to obstruction of the coronary arteries by a buildup of fatty material and plaque in arterial walls, which results in narrowing of the coronary arteries. Blood clots may also form and contribute to narrowing or closure of the coronary arteries that supply blood and oxygen to the heart. As these arteries narrow, blood flow can slow or stop, resulting in a reduced blood supply to the heart muscle. CAD may also cause a myocardial infarction (heart attack), which occurs when an area of heart muscle dies or is permanently damaged because of inadequate blood and oxygen supply to the heart muscle. Coronary artery disease may be described by the number of vessels affected, usually described as one, two, or three vessel disease. In general, individuals with single-vessel disease do well with either medical treatment or surgery. In addition to the number of vessels affected, the location and degree of narrowing will be key factors in determining the appropriate rating classification.

Risk factors for CAD include smoking, family history, male gender, hypertension, diabetes mellitus, cholesterol abnormalities, and obesity. Treatment for CAD includes lifestyle changes, medications, and surgery. Individuals with a history of CAD will not be considered for the best classes. However, if the disease is minimal, risk factors are well-controlled, the proposed insured has excellent follow-up and complies with treatment, and the CAD onset was at an older age, standard class may be possible. Age is the most important risk factor for coronary artery disease. Many older individuals can have significant disease but have only one or no unfavorable risk factors. In a very small percentage of cases, an individual applying for life insurance who has been diagnosed with CAD in their 30s are seen as uninsurable. Individuals with CAD will not be good candidates for the preferred class.

In some cases, clients may be able to receive a more favorable offer if they have had a normal stress test in the past 12 months. Individuals without CAD who have a history of two of the most common coronary artery disease risk factors (high cholesterol and elevated blood pressure), may be able to fit into the preferred class with or without medication, if their risk factors are very well-controlled and they are followed closely by their health care provider.

Today, one way carriers can be more competitive is by giving credits to offset ratings when an applicant participates in a healthy lifestyle and shows evidence of routine medical care. An example of a credit opportunity is if an applicant has elevated cholesterol that resulted in a rating, but has had a normal stress treadmill test or other cardiac testing. This could move them from a substandard class into a standard risk classification.

Breast Cancer

Breast cancer is the most common malignancy in women in the United States and is second only to lung cancer as the cause of cancer deaths. The incidence of breast cancer increases dramatically with age, and the lifetime risk of a woman developing breast cancer is 1 in 8. With the widespread use of breast cancer screening programs, the incidence of the disease is increasing, although the stage at diagnosis has become more favorable because a larger proportion of new cases are emerging that represent smaller and more localized cancers, which are more responsive to treatment. Screening and early detection has accounted for a decline in the death rate due to breast cancer in the United States. However, limited progress has been made in improving treatment for metastatic breast cancer. The mortality related to breast cancer varies depending on the stage of the cancer. Noninvasive cancer (in-situ) has a better prognosis than invasive cancers. In most cases, cancer that has spread beyond the original organ (metastatic cancer) is uninsurable. Many women know at the time of application the stage of the cancer, if any lymph nodes were involved, and the treatment. This information provides a good starting point for the underwriter, although complete medical records and the surgical pathology reports will need to be reviewed to determine the appropriate rate classification.

Prostate Cancer

Prostate cancer is the most common cancer in men and is only second to lung cancer. During a man's lifetime, a 1 in 6 chance exists of being diagnosed with prostate cancer. Prostate cancer is rarely diagnosed under the age of 40, but the risk rises with each passing decade. Most men over age 80 are diagnosed with prostate cancer when a biopsy is performed. The risk of developing prostate cancer doubles when one has a brother or father with prostate cancer. Screening for prostate cancer includes a blood test called a prostate-specific antigen (PSA) test, in addition to a digital rectal exam. The normal range of PSA varies with age. Treatment for prostate cancer may include surgery, radiation, hormone therapy, or a combination of these treatments. Regardless of treatment, the underwriter will need to review the applicant's complete medical records including the pathology reports. The risk assessment will be based on the following information: PSA values prior to treatment, date of diagnosis, pathology reports, and follow-up PSA values. The PSA value prior to and after treatment, the stage, and grade of the cancer, in addition to their age, will be the key underwriting factors in determining if the applicant is able to secure the best possible rating.

Diabetes Mellitus

Diabetes mellitus, most often is referred to as *simply diabetes*, is a syndrome of disordered metabolism, usually due to a combination of hereditary and environmental causes. It results in elevated blood sugar levels due to defects in either insulin secretion or insulin action. Type 1 diabetes mellitus is due to a loss of insulin-producing cells in the pancreas. It is sometimes referred to *juvenile diabetes* because it represents a majority of the diabetes cases in children. Type 2 diabetes is commonly associated with obesity and develops after age 30; a family history of diabetes is common in type 2. The prevalence of diabetes mellitus increases with age (mostly noninsulin diabetes or type 2 diabetes). Unrecognized diabetes mellitus and glucose intolerance are also more common in older people.

Gestational diabetes is first recognized in pregnancy and 30 percent to 50 percent of women who develop gestational diabetes will develop type 2 diabetes in 10 years. Individuals with diabetes will not qualify for the best classes. In some cases, if their disease is under excellent control and if their build, blood pressure, and cholesterol are excellent, they may be able to secure a standard class.

Cost of Insurance Related to Impairments

Life insurance allows a person to purchase protection against financial loss occurring at the time of death. By purchasing insurance, the individual participates in a pool with others who have also bought insurance. In this way, the financial loss is spread out, and the cost of providing benefits for the death claims that occur is greatly reduced. In order to be fair and equitable to as many people as possible, each individual is evaluated based on risk factors. Each receives protection at a cost that reflects their proportionate share of the expected cost of benefits for that pool. Without the risk selection process, there would be no way of knowing the risks taken on and the cost needed to make the pool work. The degree of the risk is reflected in the price the individual will pay. Not every person in a particular risk class will have the same life span, but overall, the group will have a fairly predictable life expectancy, and this grouping will give the carrier the basis to determine the premiums to be paid.

Most individuals who apply for life insurance are not in perfect health, but rather good health (standard class), and will quickly be offered polices, whereas those in excellent heath will receive the preferred class. When an applicant has medical impairments, each must be correlated with long-term mortality data relevant to that impairment.

What Information Is Needed to Complete the Qualification Process?

In order to complete the risk selection process and make an informed decision, the underwriter will need to determine the level of risk that each individual represents.

The underwriting process begins once the candidate completes an insurance application that includes important past medical history. Most companies provide a grid to agents and brokers with guidelines about what requirements are necessary based on the age of the individual applying for coverage and the amount being applied for.

Major sources of information the underwriter will need to analyze the risk will include the basic identifying information, medical information obtained from part II of the application, insurance exam, family history, build, blood pressure, laboratory findings from the blood profile and urinalysis, EKG, stress test, and the attending physician statements.

Underwriting also includes review of nonmedical information including financial details, details of occupation, avocations, and details regarding habits related to lifestyle (for example, exercise and alcohol use), and in some cases, an inspection report. The inspection report is conducted by a consumer reporting agency and typically includes information such as identity and residence verification, character, reputation, estimate of net worth and income, occupation, medical history, habits, and other personal characteristics.

Underwriting Elderly Lives

In the older ages (70 and older), the risk selection process requires additional sources of information. Medical problems, such as a decline in physical function and memory loss, are more prevalent in the older ages, and both of these conditions have been found to lead to an above aver-age mortality risk. Most carriers have developed guidelines specific to the older ages and will require specific questionnaires relating to activities. The exam will include standardized testing to detect for any memory loss that may not be noted in the medical records or time of the applica-tion. In addition, a personal telephone interview may also be conducted, which will capture information that can confirm the information previ-ously received in the application. This process is helpful in determining if the applicant has any memory difficulties. In the older ages, the profes-sional advisers may have known the applicant for a period of many years and are very familiar with their lifestyle, activities (including travel or work), and are aware of family support and social structure. Knowledge of this information could provide the underwriter with a picture of the applicants overall well being. Putting this information into a cover letter, along with the application and financial details, could make a significant positive impact on the outcome of the underwriting process.

Financial Underwriting: Does It Add Up?

Financial underwriting is a critical part of the underwriting process for each case submitted to a carrier. *Financial underwriting* is the evaluation of a prospective insured's personal or business financial background and current economic situation. Just as a loan officer must diligently analyze credit risk, so must the insurance underwriter be duly diligent in evalu-ating the insurable interest, appropriate amount of insurance coverage, including in force and applied for in all companies, and affordability. The underwriter's major objectives are as follows:

- Determine whether insurable interest exists
- Determine if the face amount is reasonable and in line with the insured's need(s)
- Determine if the amount applied for is affordable and answer the question, "Can the applicant sustain the future premium expense?"

The purpose of financial underwriting is to verify the insurable interest of a proposed insured at the time of underwriting and to prevent antiselection or speculation against the insurance company. The primary purpose of life insurance is to provide funds to help replace the economic loss, which results from the premature death of the insured person.

When a charity has been designated as beneficiary, the underwriter will need to consider the amount as it relates to past contributions. The amount of coverage should be reasonable and consistent with an ongoing pattern of support to the charity. If the donations are sporadic or one time donations, they will be regarded with caution by the underwriter. Carriers will usually look at the contributions for the past 3–5 years. In addition, the insured should have a relationship to the charity through volunteer work, paid work, or use of services. For large amounts, underwriters should be provided with certification of the contribution record from the official of the charity. The underwriter may also need to clarify that the proposed insured has adequate personal coverage.

The single most important consideration for financial underwriting of a case of any size is understanding how the sale was made. If the case is complicated, a cover letter will be instrumental in assisting the underwriter in understanding the unusual aspects of the case. The cover letter should also include the carriers involved, amounts of insurance in force and applied for, as well as coverage to be replaced. One should anticipate additional scrutiny if the arrangement is unusual. Care should be taken to explain and document the circumstances unique to the case, thereby minimizing delays and averting adverse action. In addition, the cover letter should include which professional advisers are involved (CPA, accountant, lawyer) in the financial planning.

Whether the applicant is applying for personal coverage or the need is for business, the amount of coverage available is not unlimited. Carriers set limits on the coverage a person can buy.

For personal coverage, the amount that is acceptable varies from company to company and is based principally on a person's income and net worth. Other factors that are considered are the individual's need for life insurance and amount of coverage they already have, including any business coverage (buy sell, key person). The underwriter will be concerned with signs that indicate poor personal financial health such as negative net worth, credit problems, judgments, or bankruptcies. Signs of poor financial health in a business would include operating losses, negative cash flow from operations, and adverse key financial ratios.

To determine the financial health of the applicant or company, the underwriter will request financial verification. When the amounts applied for are large, it will expedite the underwriting process if the applicant's tax returns, financial statements, or brokerage account statements are included with the application.

In the older ages, financial underwriting involves justification, just as it does in the younger ages. The rule of thumb is that need for personal insurance usually decreases with age. However, income replacement may be considered for those older than 65 because many older adults continue to work. The multiple for someone in their 30s could be 20–30 times their annual income, but for someone over age 65, it may be limited to 3–4 times their income when considering income replacement needs.

Estate planning is a common reason for purchasing life insurance in the older ages. The underwriter is often faced with not only attempting to verify whether a current estate is valued fairly, but how much value can be allowed for future growth. Underwriters will also consider the distribution of assets within the estate. Providing a copy of the estate planning analysis would be extremely helpful to the underwriter.

The multiplier used for estate valuation purposes also decreases after age 65. At these ages, the estate growth, in general, will be based on the lesser of either the life expectancy or 10 years. At ages beyond 65, up to age 80, the formula used for estate settlement cost calculation will vary by company and be based on the lesser of either half of the life expectancy or 10–15 years, with a growth factor of 6 percent. For individuals over age 80, the amount allowed will be limited to current value of the estate with a 0 growth factor.

Financial guidelines are established to support the insurance company's basic goals for profitability. The underwriter must feel comfortable that the applicant's financial position is in line with their ability to pay the premium. If the policy is not affordable and the amount is not justified, the underwriter will question and even discourage the business.

Your skills, experience, and professional education are different than those of an underwriter. As a professional adviser, you are involved in reviewing the clients' tax returns, financial statements, or other documents during the needs analysis. When it comes to the underwriting process, you can take nothing for granted when it comes to explaining the purpose of insurance and how it meets the needs of the client. Your care in illuminating and documenting any unusual situations will minimize any impending adverse actions. In conclusion, by predicting the needs of the underwriter and providing the underwriter with the most comprehensive financial picture during the initial stages of the process, you will be setting the stage for open dialogue, reducing the risk of conflict during the underwriting process, and setting the stage for the most favorable outcome.

Case Study: It's Not When to Hold or Fold—But How To
Recapturing capital from policies no longer matching goals

Key Ideas

- Life settlement versus maintaining the policy
- Negotiated underwriting

Backstory

Initially, the client's lead attorney hired The Morehead Group, for a fee, to conduct an independent, third-party analysis of the client's life insurance in relation to the estate plan. Others on the client's adviser team included the estate planning attorney, trust officer, and family office representatives, who provided a wide-range of financial experience including corporate finance, tax, financial planning, and estate planning.

The Problem

An existing $20 million life insurance policy under an endorsement split dollar plan had contractually expired, and the economic benefit costs were becoming unmanageable. There was no confidence that the pricing of the policy could be made more efficient and no clarity about alternatives in the marketplace. The client was over 80 years old, and all the advisers assumed the cost of new insurance would be prohibitively high.

A traditional level policy, which would include some immediate liquidity and strong long-term returns with increasing liquidity over time, would not sufficiently meet the client's goals. In addition, the client had an aversion to gift tax.

Put that all together and the planning team wanted to utilize insurance as an asset class, position it outside the estate, and eliminate as much gift friction as possible. However, the transaction required a "preferred" risk rating to be financially viable.

The Solution

We developed the plan to unwind the split dollar plan. After objectively evaluating the in force coverage, we recommended strategies to improve its value. Then we determined whether the policy could be settled as part of the process. The analysis favored a life settlement transaction, so the next step was to find the most efficient use of the sale proceeds—investment versus utilization for life insurance.

(continued)

(continued)

We needed to have the client medically examined, and from there, we could negotiate the underwriting result and navigate carrier and reinsurance limitations using National Financial Partners Corp's Special Case Unit.

The Results

Our negotiating success allowed us to replace the coverage with new, restructured coverage to fit the client's unique needs and goals.

The trust sold the existing policy in the secondary market, satisfied its obligations under the split dollar arrangement, and received $1 million of net proceeds. The trust used the proceeds to purchase a $1.2 million life insurance policy with an increasing death benefit up to $5 million, along with an immediate annuity to fund future insurance premiums. The increasing death benefit proceeds resulted in a 10 percent+ internal rate of return past life expectancy with no gift tax friction. Both the life insurance policy and the annuity are guaranteed by highly rated providers.

We also proposed, modified, and finalized creative structures for additional coverage, which would further address the client's needs and goals. Using a syndicate among multiple insurance carriers and a private financing structure to avoid gift tax issues, we implemented additional insurance coverage.

The trust purchased $8.5 million of life insurance increasing substantially by age 100. A portion of the premium will be gifted, with the rest privately financed by the insured. The overall transaction results in an increasing death benefit structure with a 10 percent+ internal rate of return past life expectancy.

The client and the adviser team were comfortable and in agreement with the decision-making process throughout, and they were instrumentally involved in designing the solution. It enabled them to put new policies in place with confidence, knowing that the assets would provide a valuable, additional intergenerational benefit to the heirs.

The client enjoyed attractive, long-term internal rates of return on premium dollars and an increasing death benefit as the client ages. His liquidity goals were met with tax-free liquidity outside the estate without gift tax consequences. He has achieved a diversified strategy within his overall investment portfolio.

The bank trustee fulfilled its fiduciary duty, and the attorney was credited with bringing the resources to the table.

Note that the number of bidders for a policy may be limited and proceeds from sales of similar policies may vary and may be subject to claims of creditors. Receipt of proceeds may affect eligibility for government benefits and entitlements. Prior to sale, the insured should consider the continued need for coverage on estate plans, availability of insurance, cost of comparable coverage, and tax implications. There may be high fees associated with the sale of a life settlement.

Key Questions

Advisers should be asking their clients in similar situations the following questions:

- To make sure you won't lose the value of family capital inside a life insurance policy you no longer need, shouldn't you have the policy evaluated by an expert who can present you with alternatives?
- To make sure you are receiving the most effective solutions, shouldn't you be considering only creative, customized, hand-crafted alternatives?
- To make sure you are receiving the most efficient possible life insurance pricing, shouldn't you have medical experts negotiating on your behalf?

Kenneth R. Samuelson
The Morehead Group
Charlotte, NC

Case Study: Life (Insurance) Begins at 80
Helping maximize life insurance wealth transfer advantages

Key Ideas

- Life insurance after 80
- Life insurance/annuity arbitrage
- Underwriting advocacy

Backstory #1

We have had a long relationship with Helen Mathers, her family, and their advisers. She is the 88-year-old matriarch of her family, with wealth exceeding $200 million, a few states west of us. Her will leaves everything to her grandchildren.

The Problem

Her adviser needed to transfer value to an entity outside of her estate efficiently without incurring a significant cost to her estate and wanted to know how life insurance could accomplish the goal efficiently.

The Solution

The conceptual solution involved the arbitrage between life insurance value and annuity value created by different underwriting approaches. Here's how. Mrs. Mathers loans cash, using a mid-term applicable federal rate, to a trust for the benefit of the grandchildren. The trust purchases a rated immediate annuity on her. The larger annuity distribution (due to the rating) is used not only to pay the ongoing life insurance premiums but also to cover the interest requirements of the trust's note.

At age 88, limits exist on the carriers, products, and capacity available, particularly because Mrs. Mathers also presents some medical challenges. Our underwriting objective was to have life offers at standard and annuity offers that were rated. Once we had the underwriting in place, it was necessary to time the placement of the policies to maximize the model based on the ever changing Applicable Federal Rate Index and the interest crediting rates on the annuities.

The Result

Assuming a life expectancy of age 95, the trust will have transferred over $7 million of positive value outside of her estate. The arbitrage transferred is $7,278,763— equivalent to an estate asset transfer of $36,393,813.

If Mrs. Mathers lives to age 100, the benefit outside of her estate will grow to over $12 million. The arbitrage transferred is $12,264,243—equivalent to an estate asset transfer of $61,321,217. Using guaranteed products protected this transaction, leaving carrier credit risk as the only risk exposure.

Backstory #2

Another matriarch, Mrs. Dodgson, and her family, have had an ongoing relationship with our firm for years. However, their bank-owned, multifamily office adviser saw the need for additional life insurance and recommended their in-house resources take care of the insurance placement. The family agreed with the need but asked to have our firm retained for the placement.

The Problem

Mrs. Dodgson is an 81-year-old widow with over $300 million of net worth positioned in a trust to benefit her family. Her husband had ample coverage, but she has only a total of $6 million in insurance coverage. The trust set up an interfamily loan to fund premium payments to leverage the ultimate trust value to be paid to the family.

The family advisers wanted to look at obtaining as much coverage as possible at attractive prices. We discovered many competitive products that would offer the premium efficiency necessary to hit the hurdle rates set by the advisers, but we also discovered a potential medical underwriting issue that would need the support of our underwriting advocacy programs.

The Solution

We produced a product survey of available insurance products, discussed the pros and cons of guaranteed and current assumption products, and discussed the details of the current capacity issues in acquiring large amounts of insurance coverage.

Given the medical issue, we informed Mrs. Mathers and her advisers that we would need to negotiate a favorable underwriting offer with a major carrier that could offer a large block of coverage capacity to anchor the other offers. Then, as we exhaust that supply, we move on to other carriers that offer the best remaining premium efficiency, but in smaller amounts. This way, we obtain the total amount of coverage needed without disrupting her available underwriting capacity.

(continued)

(continued)

The Result

We were able to secure $73.6 million of new coverage at favorable underwriting classifications. The premiums are $3.9 million a year—offering a double-digit return on premiums, even assuming a generous life expectancy and supporting the advisers' models. Seventy-five percent of the product was allocated to guaranteed product, and 25 percent was allocated to a current assumption product. We were able to negotiate competitive underwriting in a coordinated manner to not disturb the market capacity for an 81-year-old female, making this difficult placement look routine.

Key Questions

Advisers should be asking their clients in similar situations the following questions

- Are you aware that today longevity gains are lowering the cost of life insurance and making the advantages of life insurance tax structure available at much older ages?
- Have you considered how life insurance could shift more of your estate assets into an estate tax-free position?
- Did you know that today's life insurance policies can provide an alternative asset class that can provide very attractive returns at life expectancy?

Nat Harris
Harris, Crouch, Long, Scott & Miller, Inc.
Whitsett, NC

Case Study: Having and Eating the Proverbial Cake
Realigning life insurance capital

Key Ideas

- Capitalizing on exchanges to guaranteed death benefit universal life (GDBUL)
- Questioning the assumption of uninsurability

Backstory

Advisers who manage money for wealthy clients rely on our firm as their backroom for life insurance decisions. In many cases, we never meet the clients themselves because their financial decisions are left in the hands of a team of attorneys and accountants and our firm.

Two cases came up not long ago that demonstrate how important our knowledge can be to that team.

Problem #1

An adviser and his clients had assessed the following situation and were determined to cancel two policies on the life of the husband, while leaving the cash values for three children in the irrevocable life insurance trust (ILIT) that owned the policies.

The ILIT owned two policies on the life of the husband. Policy A was an old, $2 million universal life policy that was underfunded. It would require future annual premiums to keep it from lapsing, and the client did not want to make any further gifts to the trust. Policy B was a $2 million convertible term policy on the husband. Seven months were left in the convertibility period.

One of their children, who was one of the three beneficiaries of the trust, had developed some serious mental health problems. The parents felt that if they died and the child received too much cash, it might actually trigger self-destructive behavior and possible suicide.

Their instinct was to have the trustee cancel the UL policy and leave the cash value to be divided amongst the three beneficiaries. Their estate was large enough to take care of the disabled child without the life insurance. A special needs trust had been established for that child.

(continued)

(continued)

We were called in by the advisers to help determine what could be done with these assets to increase family capital.

Solution #1

We proposed the following alternative plan of action, which was happily embraced by the estate planning attorney and the clients. We completed the plan as follows:

A "temp" ILIT was created, in which the grantor made a loan with an interest baring note. The temp ILIT purchased the two policies from the original trust. This allowed the attorney to present a petition for modification to the original trust to the family law court. With little value in the trust, the court approved the petition. The changes addressed the special needs of the disabled child (left her out).

During the time we had the policies in the temp trust, we underwrote the wife, who turned out to be "super preferred" with the same carrier that insured the husband (term).

Using the wife's underwriting in combination with the convertibility of the husband's term policy, we had the temp trust purchase a survivor policy for the same amount of death benefit as the existing UL policy. At the same time, the existing UL was surrendered for value, and a portion of the proceeds were used to pay for the new survivor policy. The survivor policy is guaranteed for life with no further outlay.

There was enough cash left over to purchase a single life policy on the wife for an additional $1.6 million of GDBUL coverage on a one-pay basis and guaranteed for life with no further cash outlay.

The husband made a second loan with an interest note to the now modified, original trust. The modified trust purchased the new policies from the temp trust. The temp trust used those funds to repay the loan with interest. The temp trust was abandoned.

The result was $3.6 million of coverage in a modified trust versus $200,000 of cash to a trust that would distribute proceeds to the disabled child.

Problem #2

Another family had a survivorship policy in an ILIT supporting their estate plan. It had ongoing premium and gift tax obligations. The policy was no longer desired because the estate planning goals and circumstances had changed. Most policyholders and most advisers, perceiving no value to maintaining policies at considerable expense, would unhesitatingly get rid of them.

But life insurance represents family capital—cash values and death benefits— and, as they say, before the bath water is tossed, it would be smart to see if there is a baby in the tub. We asked the what-if questions. What if we exchanged the values in this policy for a paid-up universal life policy with a guaranteed death benefit?

The current policy provided close to $9 million of coverage, with a projected premium and gift tax cost over the next six years of between $1 million and $2 million, based on current earnings. We could exchange the cash value and dividends to a new, paid-up policy with nearly $6 million of coverage without a medical exam.

The big obstacle in this case was that the wife was assumed to be uninsurable due to an autoimmune disease she had battled four years prior. The husband was assumed to be a preferred health risk. It was also a reasonable assumption that insurers would have a problem taking on the wife's risk.

Even with the uninsurable rating, the exchange to a GDBUL policy was better than the current situation of future premiums and gift tax costs.

Solution #2

Don't assume—ask questions. We asked for her doctor's opinion about insurability. To our surprise, he explained that her condition had reversed, and her medications were now prophylactic only. He wrote a narrative summary of her health history and prognosis, complete with supporting lab and test result documentation, which we presented to the underwriters. We learned that she was not only insurable but she was not even "rated." We proceeded to investigate the conversion solution. She was reluctant to take the medical exam because she had had so much medical trauma in the recent past. Eventually she completed an exam at her attending physician's office. The result was a "preferred" risk. The policy was actually worth $9 million—no loss compared to the original policy—with no additional premiums or gift tax obligations. The savings to this family were between $1 million and $2 million.

(continued)

(continued)

Key Questions

Advisers should be asking their clients in similar situations the following questions:

- Before you surrender any life insurance policies that you feel you no longer need, have you evaluated the policies to see if you are unknowingly throwing away any family capital remaining in those policies?
- Are you aware that medical advances have created a new underwriting landscape in which past insurability issues—your age or your health—may no longer be an obstacle?

Paul Jablon
The Jablon Group
Los Angeles, CA

Case Study: Wealth Transfer Efficiency
New funding strategy for existing trusts

Key Ideas

- Alternative wealth transfer strategies
- Life insurance funding for trusts
- Negotiated underwriting and independent product selection

Backstory

Our company, Innovative Benefits Consulting, Inc. (IBC), markets to affluent clients through their existing advisers at accounting firms and banks. During an in-house briefing to one of our bank alliances on using funded trusts to purchase insurance, a question came up about a bank client's existing funded irrevocable trust. Although the briefing centered on funded credit shelter trusts, one of the bank officers applied the information to a broader issue, and the answer led to an introduction to a situation in which the clients fit the fact pattern.

In 1907, Michael Sanborn's grandfather established a trust with the First Fairplay Bank. Since that time, the Sanborn family members have been loyal customers to the bank and have an existing revocable trust with the bank valued at $3 million. Michael (age 76) and his wife Jill (age 72) also own over $10 million in a closely-held, now publicly traded, family business and have $4 million in a brokerage account. Michael refuses to divest his ownership of the family business stock and has elected to maintain his holding outside of the revocable trust.

The Sanborn's children are grown with families of their own. Each of their children is dependent upon annual $24,000 gifts for ongoing living expenses. Michael and Jill have 13 grandchildren and have been gifting $24,000 to minor's trusts for their benefit. In 2001, they used their $1 million unified credit in gifting their vacation home to a qualified personal residence trust.

Michael's mother, Mary, created a trust at her death in 1979 that permits the bank to sprinkle income to Michael and his children. This trust has a $5 million value, and the bank is trustee. Given the children's need for income, the trustee has generally sprinkled income to them equally each year. Michael also has a limited testamentary power of appointment over this trust, and the trust will distribute directly to Michael's issue should he not exercise the power.

(continued)

(continued)

What If?

Together with the bank's senior trust officer, we identified several key facts about Michael and Jill's estate that matched up to our "fact pattern to look for:"

- Taxable estate over $17 million
- No life insurance within estate plan
- A large irrevocable trust is currently in place
- Children's continual need of income and support
- Concentrated holding of family business

The bank had played an important part in helping Michael and Jill plan their estate disposition. At a regularly scheduled investment meeting, the trust adviser mentioned that they had been thinking more about their estate planning goals and introduced an idea he developed with us. What if they used Mary's trust as an estate planning tool?

The conventional ILITs previously considered to provide the annual gift income the children need have created cash flow issues for the children. The trust adviser introduced the idea that Mary's trust could purchase a second-to-die policy on Michael and Jill. Mary's trust distributes about 3 percent in income to the children. The trust also is allocated 75 percent equity and 25 percent bond. Consistent with total-return theory, the adviser wanted to find out what 2 percent ($100,000) could buy in death benefit for the trust. Michael and Jill thought the idea had potential and gave the trust adviser permission to arrange an introduction to our IBC team to explore possibilities.

Implementation

We began working with Michael and Jill to obtain medical information and demonstrated how IBC is able to independently shop the cost of life insurance among many high quality companies.

Based on the underwriting results, we determined that an $8 million joint policy would require a $105,000 premium. The cash payments were derived from sale of stock, using capital gain to fund premiums. Additionally, Michael needed to sign a disclaimer over the limited power to appoint any of the insurance proceeds.

Internal rates of return (IRR) of the insurance policy show that for life expectancy, the IRR would generate in excess of 15 percent return.

Key Questions

Advisers should be asking their clients in similar situations the following:

- If the tax structure of life insurance could be applied in this situation to more efficiently achieve your goals, wouldn't you want to know about it?
- If we can collaborate with independent life insurance professionals to assure the best combination of pricing, underwriting, and product design, wouldn't you want us to?

Greg Steliotes
Innovative Benefits Consulting, Inc.
Pittsburgh, PA

Case Study: The Disciplined Entrepreneur
Educating clients in their best interests

Key Ideas

- Equal versus fair in estate planning
- Life insurance role in asset equalization
- LIT

Backstory

Ray Pennington owns a very successful regional restaurant supply company called PRS, Inc., founded decades ago and nurtured on entrepreneurial grit. A few years ago he began contemplating his eventual exit from the business and asked his accountant what steps would be necessary to prepare for that day—even though he was not willing to commit to a definite timetable.

Our firm has worked with his accountant on several family business transition situations over the years, and he suggested to Ray that we all set aside a few hours together to talk through the steps conceptually. Ray agreed to the meeting, and what follows is the content of that conceptual discussion.

The Problem

The meeting began with Ray explaining that, no doubt, PRS, Inc. would be a candidate for acquisition by a national wholesaler. But, although he wanted to keep the family's options open, he explained that his children had grown up with the feeling that the company was actually one more sibling at the dinner table, and selling it would be hard for everyone.

All of them had worked at PRS after school and during summers, and two of them had worked up to management positions. The remaining two children had opted for other careers—one is a special education teacher, and the other owns a dental practice. But all four take for granted that PRS is the family legacy.

His concern was how to equally divide something that was inherently indivisible.

After listening, we began by telling Ray that virtually all our clients embrace the goal of equality among children. It seems natural, fair, and easy to say—and may be the right place to start. But no law exists that demands that when disposing of one's estate to the next generation, all children must be treated equally. And, in practical terms, equality is not easy to implement, as Ray intuitively grasped.

Our role as financial advisers is not to second guess a client's stated goal of equality but, instead, to confirm that the statement is a product of careful thought, not just an assumption taken for granted. Sometimes clients say "equal" when they really mean "fair."

Perfect equality, of course, would demand that each child receive an equal undivided interest in each asset of the estate, specifically including the family business. Virtually nothing could be better designed to destroy family relationships in the next generation.

We wanted to show Ray the issues equality raises and the strategies to resolve them, so he could make informed decisions and execute the plan over the right timeframe to assure its success. And part of that role is to ask tough questions and get emotionally charged issues on the table so they do not come up later to sabotage the plan.

The Alternatives

When a family business is the major asset in the estate, and when some children are active in the business whereas others remain inactive or engaged in other careers, three main strategies exist to achieve the goal of equality.

- Get the inactive children out of the business, and give those children nonbusiness assets of substantially equivalent value
- Get the inactive children out of the main business, but keep the inactive children peripherally involved in the business
- Keep the inactive children directly involved in the business, but limit their power to affect management decisions

It has been our experience over 38 years of developing business transition strategies for clients that the best solution is to eliminate the inactive children from the business and provide those children other nonbusiness assets of equivalent value in lieu of interests in the business.

If that is not possible, we think it is critical that the inactive children be only peripherally involved in the business, perhaps as lessor of one or more business assets. If neither of those strategies is available, as a last resort, clients might decide to keep the inactive children directly involved in the business, but limit such children's powers. However, this last resort is likely to cause almost as many problems as would have occurred had there been no planning.

(continued)

(continued)

In such situations, business financial strategy eventually conflicts with personal financial strategies. Business growth feeds on reinvesting profits, whereas personal needs argue for distributions. When business decisions come down to shareholder voting, nobody wins unless everybody wins, and when somebody loses, everybody loses.

When we probed deeper into the financial situations and relationship ties in the next generation, Ray realized that as close as his family is, plenty of room exists for disagreements over what is equal and what is fair. He saw it as only a matter of time before equality—achieved through the business alone—could become divisive.

We added that preempting future conflicts with a comprehensive financial, business transition and estate plan is only one course of action. A parallel plan for the transfer of family beliefs, values, and commitment to stewardship of the family legacy would do the rest.

The Solution

The easiest way for Ray to give inactive children nonbusiness assets of substantially equivalent value is *segregation of assets*. Ideally, to implement the segregation of assets strategy, Ray would have available to his estate assets having a value equal to the value of the shares of the business to be received by the active children. Equality is achieved, and conflicts between the needs of the business controlled by the active children and the personal financial needs of nonactive children can be avoided.

In this case, the value of the business was too high compared to the remaining assets to be segregated. The second option to consider is to *create cash*, either within or outside the Pennington estate, and to distribute all or a portion of that cash to the inactive children in amounts that achieve equality with the value of the shares of the business going to the active children.

The most efficient way to create cash is the effective use of life insurance policy design and tax structure. Several ways to apply life insurance to the goal of creating cash come readily to mind.

The first is life insurance payable to the estate. Ray could acquire insurance payable upon his death to his estate. Following his death, the personal representative could use the insurance proceeds to equalize the amount of assets distributed to the active and inactive children. The strategy has the advantage of simplicity. However, the strategy exposes the insurance proceeds to probate, risk of creditor's claims, and estate tax, thereby raising the effective cost of the insurance.

Alternatively, Ray could buy a policy on his life naming as beneficiary the inactive children and gift the policy to the inactive children. The inactive children could also apply for the policy on his life, with Ray gifting to them the amounts necessary to pay the premiums. If the children apply for the policy, Section 2035 of the Internal Revenue Code (IRC) might apply depending upon the degree to which the premiums are traceable directly to the client.

A third scenario involves the use of an irrevocable insurance trust. Ray establishes an irrevocable insurance trust that provides, upon Ray's death, the trustee (in coordination with the activities of the family's personal representative), distributions to the inactive children the amount necessary to equalize the value of the assets received by active and inactive children from both the estate and trust. The balance of the trust estate, if any, could be distributed to the active children. Properly drawn, such a trust could create "perfect justice" in terms of equality of amounts and could eliminate the insurance from Ray's estate, allowing it to pass to beneficiaries income tax- and estate tax-free.

Another consideration is the *impact of sequence of death*. Often a business will pass to the children of the founder only upon the later death of the founder's surviving spouse, and during the interim between the death of the founder and his or her spouse, those children who were active in the business will become more active. Equalizing value, therefore, demands not only appreciation of an adherence to the goal of equality, but also a determination of the time of which such analysis is to take place.

The Result

The meeting allowed us to fulfill our responsibility to help Ray Pennington see and understand the sources of postdeath tensions typical of family business succession. Leaving aside all the numbers and graphs and spreadsheets that will eventually help define the plan, the educational approach made him comfortable with our expertise and our willingness to provide him with every resource he will need. Ray now approaches continuity planning in the thoughtful and disciplined manner that will assure his goals.

(continued)

(continued)

Key Questions

Advisers should be asking their clients in similar situations the following questions:

- Now that your company has achieved such success, do you know what you need to do to start climbing your next mountain?
- In thinking about the eventual distribution of your estate, how do you view what is equal versus what is fair for your children?
- Do you have a family legacy statement that assures you pass your values along with your assets to future generations of your family?

James W. Monteverde
The Monteverde Group, LLC
Pittsburgh, PA

Life Insurance Policy Management and Advice 5

In the 1950s through the mid-1970s, life insurance was a very stable industry without much innovation. Life insurance policies were purchased primarily to give policyholders long-term security. Except for changing beneficiaries when needed, the policies remained in a box of family records.

For many American industries, planned obsolescence has been an acceptable manufacturing strategy for many decades. In the 1950s, auto manufacturers completed massive model redesigns every three years as the ideal balance between the cost of retooling and the need to sell new cars to repeat customers. On the consumers' side, an expectation was deeply implanted that they should buy a new car every three years. And coincidentally, it took about three years for American cars to develop major problems that were too expensive to repair.

Obviously no one was monitoring the impact of this policy on the environment, but replacement made for a strong economy and good capitalism. Today we have grown used to an even more amazing replacement strategy in the technology sector, where breakthroughs occur so quickly there is hardly time for planned obsolescence. But the insurance industry always maintained a different standard, and *replacement* was, for a very long time, a very dirty word.

That's because old school life insurance is, by design, a buy-and-hold investment. Policies are structured to increase in benefit over time. As long as companies remain financially stable, they will meet the contractual obligations of the policy. And because the life insurance value increases with time, what good would it do to replace an existing product with one that was starting all over from a lower level of value?

In that environment, an agent who suggested replacing policies was probably not acting in the policyholder's interest. The new policy simply represented a new commission, and clients remained uninformed about what they were giving up instead of what they were gaining or about the potential trade-offs. If the justification for replacement was simply the need for additional coverage, that goal could have been accomplished without sacrificing policies.

But in the economic environment of the late 1970s and 1980s, factors such as interest rates and product innovation led to widespread replacement of policies. In many cases, the replacement was warranted and prudent. The life insurance advisers were acting in their clients' best interests. But it was also a time abuse by unscrupulous agents, managers, and company executives.

Today's life insurance products are still designed as long-term financial instruments; but it has become clear that the economic environment can change quickly, and clients need to respond quickly. Sometimes replacement is warranted because client circumstances change, and previous sound decisions are suddenly no longer sound.

In that environment, "buy-and-hold" does not mean "forget about it"—it means buy and review. Life insurance has moved out of the separate box it once resided—a unique financial tool devoted to a simple and universal risk. It is now defined and treated as a capital management tool—providing unique growth potential through its tax structure, risk management value, and multigenerational capital.

What has changed from the old school approach is that a new component has been added to the life insurance industry: long-term proactive service. The life insurance industry has always been able to claim a high service standard, but not a proactive one.

Managed capital means life insurance policies should be reevaluated in the context of periodic financial planning and whenever client circumstances and decision-making factors change significantly. The review should determine whether the product is still the suitable solution to the problem and whether the policy and the company issuing it are performing to the benchmarks set at the last review.

Unfortunately, evaluation of life insurance policies is typically not a focus of the review procedures of any of the advisory professions. The subject generally comes up only when clients call to get their advisers' input. They become involved in life insurance decision-making and want the objective opinion of a trusted adviser. In many cases, the decision will already have been made conceptually, and they are really looking for a quick confirmation that they are not making a mistake.

That puts advisers immediately into a dilemma. You do not have a full picture of the components of the decision. You do not want to give a knee-jerk response. But you also know your client does not want your input to prove so complicated that the decision-making process goes off track. If the decision involves the replacement of one policy by another, your antenna should go up.

The life insurance industry offers you some help in making a quick response that does not fall into the knee-jerk category. The general position of the industry is that most replacements cannot be justified when all factors are considered. In addition to the financial considerations that might arise from illustrations, a policyholder must understand that replacement can include the following:

- New sales loads
- New company rights to challenge a death claim during contestability and suicide periods
- Changes in age or health that increase the risk
- Changes in policy loan rates
- Less favorable nonforfeiture values and guarantees
- Loss of grandfathered rights
- Gain in policy values for income tax purposes
- Potential surrender charges for replacing the policy

In other words, taken together, whatever financial gains might be anticipated by the replacement of one policy for another may also involve significant trade-offs. The loss of these may outweigh the potential gains.

But that general statement still leaves ample room to justify replacing a policy, and you can help your clients by alerting them to specific conceptual factors and financial measures that must be considered.

The first level of evaluation should identify what changes in client goals and circumstances have brought the original life insurance policy into question. These changes should be articulated and quantified as objectives, integrated with the client's overall financial plan. If the objectives cannot be met by the existing planning, then alternatives must be weighed.

Once the objectives are clear, the next step is to investigate whether the current insurance company is willing to modify the policy to meet those objectives. If so, the objectives are likely to be met with fewer trade-offs than would occur with a new policy. If not, then replacement must be considered.

The analysis of the relative merits of policy replacement can begin with recognizing the reduction in cash surrender value that will result from the acquisition costs associated with the new policy. This can be determined by comparing cash surrender value of the original policy immediately before replacement and the cash surrender value of the proposed policy immediately after the replacement. As a caution, these values will not be accurate if taken from an illustration, which reflects end-of-year values and should be obtained directly from the companies' policyholder service departments.

The next step involves comparison of the terms and projected performance among the proposed and existing policies. Critical to this evaluation are factors such as the following:

- The timeframe required for the proposed policy cash surrender values and death benefits to exceed those in the current policy
- The crediting or yield rates being assumed in the proposed alternative policies and the justification for these assumptions
- Differences in the structure of the policy and the addition of riders
- Comparison of both the length of guarantees at illustrated premium levels and differences in the amount of premium necessary to maintain guaranteed levels for life

Tax issues must then be reviewed. Is there potential taxable gain and how will it be handled? The policyholder should determine that the proposed policy will qualify as life insurance for income tax purposes, whether a policy exchange will be utilized to preserve basis, and how policy loans will be handled.

Also, over the years, tax law change has altered some important tax benefits for life insurance policies, and each time, these benefits have been preserved in existing policies through grandfathering. Depending on the issue date of the current policy, these grandfathered benefits may be sacrificed by replacement. The insurance adviser should supply a list of these grandfathered benefits and the issue dates affecting them.

Finally, the financial strength of the respective companies represented by the current and proposed policies must be examined based on the criteria recommended in the previous section.

This procedure should eliminate the dilemma previously posed and allow you to give your clients the objective input they are looking for. The general statement is designed to prevent imprudent replacement of existing policies. Prudent replacement disregards that statement only when the proposed policy passes such tests as the ones outlined.

Life Insurance Advice

Two kinds of risk exist for advisers giving advice to their clients about life insurance.

The Adviser's Dilemma

Any time an adviser steps outside of his or her own disciplines on behalf of his or her clients, even a seemingly unimportant detail that is missed or mistaken creates a vector that may lead clients off course. Conversely, advisers might hesitate to address problems for their client just because they lie outside their own discipline. In either scenario, clients could make uninformed decisions, and the result could be financial loss or lost opportunity for the clients, and certainly loss of the relationship, or worse.

Clients expect their advisers to protect their interests. They expect a high level of expertise. And they expect responsiveness—proactively. But they may be hazy about lines drawn between professions or suspicious when their advisers extend their practices beyond traditional boundaries.

How many accountants, attorneys, and trustees believe they can offer due diligence or due care in the life insurance decisions their clients have to make?

Clients may simply want opinions, but the weight of an adviser's opinion in such circumstances may tip the balance to endorsement in spite of oral and written disclaimers, limitations on the scope of services, and constraints on the applicability of advice.

When an adviser has a fiduciary responsibility as a trustee, responsibilities may be governed by the Uniform Prudent Investor Act, which sets standards and procedures for all trust investments. Much of the life insurance purchased as a funding device for estate tax liabilities is held in trusts. This raises the liability bar for advisers who serve as trustees, or advise clients who are trustees, even higher than that of the insurance agent.

The act specifies a trustee duty to the beneficiaries to make and implement decisions concerning the retention and disposition of original investments. If a trustee undertakes an investment outside his or her skill and experience, the failure to delegate its execution to a qualified expert may constitute a breach of trust. With life insurance, trustee responsibility cannot be limited to policy performance. Unlike other trust investments, numerous noninvestment issues and tax consequences need to be dealt with.

Can the trustee claim a committee of beneficiaries is so qualified? Probably not. What about a life insurance agent? An agent may be qualified to make recommendations, but how should the agent's financial gain be factored in? Compounding that difficulty, a wide variation exists among agents about what long-term service commitment remains after the initial decision. From the agent's perspective, such review work may be considered noncompensated. Worse, the agent may have left the business, and the policy now has *orphan* status, a limbo realm within the life insurance company.

Adviser liability in the life insurance arena is an issue without easy parallels and precedents. No adviser wants to be the lawsuit to set that precedent, but being overcautious carries as many liabilities.

Common Ground

Resolving this adviser dilemma requires moving up a level and realizing that the role of life insurance has changed as much as the roles of advisers.

Life insurance has traditionally been considered and treated as a buy-and-hold investment. But many took the word *hold* to mean *ignore*. That proved potentially disastrous because many of the cash accumulation policies purchased in the 1980s failed to perform to projections within 10 years.

In the past two decades, the need to more frequently and consistently reevaluate life insurance for suitability and performance in relation to clients' overall financial goals altered the buy-and-hold perspective. Today, life insurance has to be viewed as family or corporate capital (in the form of a life insurance contract) and has to be managed as a capital asset over years, decades, and even generations.

And that concept is the common ground among professional disciplines that come together over life insurance decisions. Every member of the advisory team has a role, defined in terms of managing the capital represented by the life insurance contract, from designing the policy variables to the client's plan, to the accounting processes and legal structures and trustee oversight.

Since effective life insurance decision-making among affluent clients and corporations inevitably requires participation by multiple advisers, one safeguard can be found in creating working standards for the advisory team. The first responsibility of advisers is to make sure the team truly pulls together to help clients manage family and corporate capital in the form of life insurance.

Case Study: A "Secret Word" Worth a Lot More Than $100
How small details can affect generation after generation

Key Ideas

- Multigenerational wealth transfer
- Repairing inadvertent planning gaps

Backstory

We were called in by a family to offer advice on the family's multigenerational wealth transfer strategies. The family founded a food manufacturing company late in the 19ᵗʰ century that has become a national institution and whose products are enjoyed globally. To respect the family's privacy, they are referred to here only in terms of generations (G1, G2, and so forth).

G1 created a number of trusts some 60 years ago that pay income to G2 during their lifetimes and, after the last to die of G2, for an additional 21 years to G3. The income interest terminated after 21 years to comply with the rule against perpetuities, which limits the period to, at the latest, 21 years after the death of the last identifiable individual living at the time the interest was created. At the end of the perpetuities period, the trust corpus passes to charity. Our role was to advise whether this arrangement remained suitable and efficient in light of current wealth transfer opportunities.

The Problem

We began by studying the trust documents and located one problem in the wording that actually put the plan at risk. The trust referred to the G2 beneficiaries as *children* rather than *issue* of the founder.

The impact of that obscure and seemingly minor detail meant that if one of the G2 members died, his own children would be the last beneficiaries of the trust for the remaining 21 years or their deaths—the difference of the definition of *children* and *issue*. If one of the G3 beneficiaries died before the trust passed to charity, the income interest of the deceased beneficiary would cease and not be paid to his or her issue—G4.

The risk was greatest to one line of G2. In the other lines, either no G3 children existed, or the G3 children were considerably older and already well-established financially and would not be affected significantly if the income interest terminated.

The Solution

Because the trusts were irrevocable, we proposed a strategy to manage the risk to G3 and G4 outside the trusts. The solution was simple—G2 could fund life insurance premiums to insure G3 for the benefit of G4. The founder's intention of passing assets to G3, and then from G3 to future generations, could be sustained in an efficient manner from legal, financial, and tax points of view.

Because G2 had extensive taxable gifts and planned on using their full annual exclusion gifts each year, gifting premiums would be subject to both gift and generation-skipping taxes. To avoid this result, the plan was structured as a split dollar arrangement. In addition, because one of the members of G3 was uninsurable, the eldest member of G3 was insured as a surrogate for the others.

At the time, the policies were funded for a projected 15 years with the intention of terminating the split dollar arrangement in the 21 year. Eleven years into the plan, however, some family financial disagreements arose that required modification to the original premium funding structure.

In addition, by the end of the eleventh year, the IRS had issued extensive new regulations concerning split dollar arrangements that would have made the resurrection of the grandfathered, original split dollar arrangement impossible. This required restructuring the arrangement in its entirety while preserving the benefits of the original plan.

The Results

Our discovery of an unfortunate word choice in the trust documents, dating back some six decades, led to an alternative strategy that preserved the intention of the founding generation to transfer family assets across multiple generations.

Then, changing family circumstances, combined with changing tax regulations, led to a second strategy to bring the plan current with the family's feelings and current with the tax and financial environment.

One lesson that was confirmed by this case is that the devil is, indeed, in the details. However, an even more important lesson emerges—planning is a dynamic process, not a static event that must be reviewed regularly. In short, planning is never completed.

(continued)

(continued)

Yesterday's solutions, however sound they may have been, can become today's problems. And, in turn, today's solutions, based on current assumptions, current circumstances, and current regulations, have to be adaptable to change, or they will become tomorrow's problems.

In every professional discipline—legal, accounting, financial, insurance, trusts—the commitment to ongoing monitoring, modification, and communication has to meet the highest standards.

Key Questions

Advisers should be asking their clients in similar situations the following questions:

- When your family's estate planning was first initiated, what were the guiding philosophy and the primary intentions, and are they still the same?
- How long has it been since your earlier planning strategies have been thoroughly analyzed in light of current family intentions and changes is the tax and economic environment, and how long is too long?

Sam Radin
National Madison
New York, NY

Case Study: Controlling the Cost of Time
Short- and long-term transfer tax strategies

Key Ideas

- Role of term insurance
- Value of term conversion
- Advantages of the secondary market

Backstory

Our firm was introduced to Alex Janson by a third party, and we initiated discussions about his plan to transfer his considerable assets at his death. For many years, Mr. Janson had been a tax adviser, but he left private practice to found a new specialized financial services firm. The firm was very successful and later was acquired by a national financial services institution. Mr. Janson had achieved a very high level of financial success by the time we began our planning discussions.

What we discovered when we first looked at the information his advisers supplied us was very surprising. Despite his own legal, tax, and financial experience, he had undertaken only minimal planning all these years. As a result, the ultimate transfer of his financial success was at considerable tax risk. Apparently, in the area of wealth transfer planning, he was a perfect example of, "Do as I say, not as I do."

Sadly, not long after we first met with him—and before any planning steps could be implemented—he died suddenly. The time required to discuss the risks, let alone resolve them, vanished with his death.

Thanks to the unlimited marital deduction, the transfer tax liability at Mr. Janson's death was $0. However, the transfer tax liability on what was now Mrs. Janson estate was 55 percent based on estate tax rates at the time.

The executor and trustee of the Janson estate was Mr. Coffield, one of Janson's associates in the acquired financial services firm and a great personal friend of the family. Of course, because Alex Janson's life had a huge impact in his business and civic community, Mr. Coffield's social duties alone after the death were extensive. Because the estate passed without tax consequences to Mrs. Janson, future wealth transfer issues were not at the top of anyone's agenda.

(continued)

(continued)

The transfer issues had not been at the top of Mr. Janson's agenda either, and his death made it all the more important that they be placed there. That was our role, but it should also have been the role of other advisers who were aware of the financial stakes. No one wants to intrude at such a sensitive time, but what would that sensitivity be worth if something should happen to Mrs. Janson?

Problem #1

Mrs. Janson's estate was estimated at roughly $100 million, and, based on the 55 percent estate tax rate, when she dies, her heirs will owe the federal government roughly $55 million in estate taxes.

We assured Mr. Coffield that, *in time*, her estate tax liability could be reduced and potentially even eliminated with sophisticated wealth transfer tax and funding strategies. But the risk lay in that two-word phrase *in time*. If time ran out on her, as it had run out on her husband, the result for her family could be disastrous. What assets would the heirs use to write that $55 million check?

Solution #1

The first priority for the Janson estate was to gain control of the time required to complete the wealth transfer plan. We recommended creating an immediate liquid asset to meet the tax liability if Mrs. Janson were to die unexpectedly before that plan became reality.

The most efficient asset to "buy some time" is a guaranteed death benefit provided by a term life insurance policy. In effect, the estate would now have a "first aid kit" ready for a possible injury.

Mr. Coffield agreed that the concept of buying time was critical. However, he didn't believe someone in her mid-70s would qualify for or could afford $55 million of insurance coverage. Here's how we resolved the doubts.

By submitting applications to several carriers, we were able to negotiate $55 million of coverage for $275,000 annual premium, and Mrs. Janson received a preferred risk underwriting rating from the life insurance companies.

After analyzing cash flow needs, it was decided that $200,000 a year would be budgeted for premium payments, which would provide a $40 million liquid asset against transfer tax liabilities. The remainder would be funded by other estate assets.

The $40 million of coverage was layered in two term policies to allow more flexibility in managing the asset—guaranteed renewable for 10 and 15 years, respectively, and convertible up to specified ages in each policy.

Meanwhile, the planning effort to reduce estate tax liabilities by asset transfer and gifting techniques was underway. The cost of time before the life insurance "first aid kit" was purchased had been a simple gamble for the Janson family—either $0 or $55 million. Now the cost of time became a simple risk management plan at $200,000 a year for up to 15 years.

Problem #2

The Janson estate was protected against the risk of Mrs. Janson's death, but not yet completely protected against the possible loss of her health after 15 years.

Guaranteed renewable term insurance provides continuing coverage every year of the term at the same premium without proof of insurability. The death benefit is now a managed asset that will be applied to an expected liability. But these life insurance assets could also play other roles in the estate plan for the rest of Mrs. Janson's life. Does it make sense to just let that asset run out?

What if she lives beyond the 10-year and then 15-year terms, but her health changes so that underwriting for new term policies raises the cost prohibitively? Or what if she becomes uninsurable?

We posed the questions hypothetically, but that is exactly what happened. Six months into the policy, she received an adverse diagnosis.

Fortunately, treatment has made her prognosis positive, but unfortunately, she is now uninsurable. So now if she lives longer than the 10 and 15 years of guaranteed renewable life insurance provided by her policies, the value of the asset goes from $40 million of death benefit to $0.

Solution #2

Although the addition of new insurance became unavailable, the term conversion option remained open. Life insurance companies allow term policies to be converted to permanent policies for a specified time period without additional underwriting.

For the purpose of conversion, her adverse health event had no impact. Mrs. Janson was still considered a preferred risk. Although we could still control time as

(continued)

(continued)

long as conversion remained an option, we needed to carefully analyze the value of the insurance asset beyond the term coverage and weigh it against the higher costs of permanent insurance.

Most consumers think of term policies as more affordable than permanent policies. Here we have a different issue from affordability. Mrs. Janson valued affordability initially, but now she saw the value of lifetime coverage to support the goals of the wealth transfer plan.

She also had an adviser with a penchant for in-depth financial modeling, who extensively compared the cost and benefit of letting the term run out versus converting the term to permanent insurance. The conversion raised the annual premium by a factor of five—from $86,000 to $437,000 roughly.

With permanent policies, cash accumulation in the policy can be used to manage premium levels over time, so his comparisons were very complex. In the end, his verdict was to convert the 10-year policy, which was accomplished on the last day of the conversion period. The second policy has a longer time period for conversion and will get the same detailed analysis, on an ongoing basis, to determine if and when conversion is the more efficient use of the life insurance asset.

Added Opportunity

We also explained that nonconverted term life insurance has no market value after the conversion right expires. But conversion preserves this value as a potential cost recovery, because her permanent insurance assets have value in the secondary market.

That value can be captured in a life settlement transaction, transforming the death benefit asset into an asset to be put to use during Mrs. Janson's lifetime.

Flexibility is always valuable in long-term planning because increased flexibility means increased control. Now Mrs. Janson has established a third option on top of the choice to let the insurance run out or keep it for her lifetime.

Lessons Learned

Everyone involved in the case appreciated not only being alerted to a potential problem, one that had no way of getting attention in the short term. But equally important was that the short-term solution could be achieved with no difficulty during an otherwise unsettling and emotional time.

Our strong recommendation to put in place as soon as possible an estate planning band aid turned out to be prophetic when the adverse health event occurred. The goal was to regain control of time, which had been lost with the untimely death of Alex Janson, and both the goal and the wisdom of the goal were realized.

That health event, in turn, set in motion the ability to convert an asset with a limited shelf life into a permanent asset, as well as adding potential for favorably transforming the value of the asset again in a later sale if future circumstances warrant it.

Key Questions

Advisers should be asking their clients in similar situations the following questions:

- If you have secured your spouse against estate tax liability at your death with the unlimited marital deduction, shouldn't you also secure family assets against the estate tax that must be paid at your spouse's death?
- Have you considered the value of term insurance as more than short-term protection, but also as an interim step to greater coverage without time limits?
- If comprehensive estate planning seems too involved right now, shouldn't you at least look into a what-if estate plan that tells you where your risks lie?
- When was the last time you revisited your estate plan in the context of one spouse's death?
- Your estate planning goal is to first protect your spouse financially in the event of your death, but have you considered the result if your spouse dies first?
- Have you reviewed your survivorship policies since your spouse's death to evaluate new planning issues and opportunities in your insurance portfolio?

Steve Hubbard
Innovative Benefits Consulting, Inc.
Pittsburgh, PA

Case Study: Charitable Goals Meet Family Goals
Resolving the inherent financial conflict between family and charitable legacies

Key Ideas

- Charitable lead annuity trust (CLAT)
- Replacing the value of estate assets with life insurance

Backstory

Jeanette Matson contacted us at the recommendation of her friend, who is one of our current clients. She has consistently made charitable giving a priority in her life, donating the income she receives from a bond portfolio with assets totaling $1 million.

At 60, Mrs. Matson had decided to increase her charitable commitment as well as make arrangements to leave a portion of her estate to this charity. She became frustrated that these good intentions were at odds with her goals for her heirs. She had not been informed of all her options and had not known the right questions to ask.

The Problem

Increasing her charitable gift required using the principal of her bond portfolio, and she would like to preserve this asset for her heirs.

The Decision Process

We set up a discovery meeting to introduce her to our approach to charitable planning and our resources within the firm and through our relationship with PartnersFinancial. We asked her to bring her accountant and attorney to create a "think tank" atmosphere and look for uncommon solutions tailored to her situation. In our experience, the best solutions are created and implemented when advisers work together as a team.

In this meeting, we discussed Mrs. Matson's current estate and financial plans. We explained how the seemingly conflicting goals of increasing charitable gifts from the bond portfolio and preserving the value of the portfolio for her heirs could both be achieved by integrating them into the appropriate trust vehicle. She liked the concept and appreciated that her other advisers were available to endorse the concept.

The Solution

We worked with her attorney to draft a CLAT. Under her accountant's supervision, Mrs. Matson then transferred the bond portfolio into the CLAT, which is obligated to make regular payments to a charity for a specific period of time. We next implemented a secured principal life annuity inside the CLAT to enhance the annual charitable gift. Under the attorney's supervision, she transferred the funds from the bond portfolio to a single premium immediate annuity and a life insurance policy. This structure increased the client's annual gift by 25 percent and guarantees annual cash flow to the client's charity.

Results

By working with the client's attorney and utilizing the CLAT, the client transferred $1 million out of her estate, which reduced her estate tax liability. This structure, at the advice of her accountant, allowed the client to increase her annual charitable gift by transferring the bond portfolio into the secured principal life annuity.

Once the term of years for the charity expires, beneficiaries will receive a fixed income stream until the client's death. These payments are not subject to gift taxes. Upon the client's death, beneficiaries will receive $1 million free of income tax and estate tax.

The charity received more value from this solution than it would have from her bond portfolio directly. Her heirs received more from this approach than they would have by inheriting the bond portfolio directly.

Key Questions

Advisers should be asking their clients in similar situations the following questions:

- Would you be interested in increasing your charitable gifts if it could be done with no negative impact on your children's inheritance?
- Would you be interested in strategies to increase the yield on your fixed income portfolio?
- Would you like to learn a more efficient way to make gifts to charity that could allow you to increase the amount of your annual gifts?

Robert Schechter
Schechter Wealth Strategies
Birmingham, Michigan

Case Study: From Tax Savings to the Greater Good
Applying life insurance tax structure for saving and giving

Key Ideas

- Tax advantages of a CLAT
- Life insurance tax structure applied to a CLAT

Backstory

Benjamin Easton was referred to our firm by a CPA with whom we had worked in the past. Mr. Easton was a successful, self-employed money manager who had an unusually high earned income in a year (over $5 million) and was looking for creative ideas to shelter income from taxes. Any additional benefits derived from income tax savings strategies were welcome but not a primary need.

The Solution

We initially suggested a 412(i) pension plan,[1] which gave the client a large income tax deduction coupled with a potential death benefit. The tax deduction appealed to him, but as a very experienced investor, he was not enamored of putting a significant contribution into a fixed annuity paying a minimal rate of interest.

We then shifted gears and presented an alternative strategy that excited Mr. Easton once he saw potential inherent possibilities for boosting charitable and financial goals. We proposed the implementation of a CLAT.

The concept was to initially create a CLAT which would primarily invest in a variable life insurance policy with a minimum death benefit, and an ILIT. We presented different charitable payout amounts, term of years, and the corresponding benefits to his family based on an initial contribution of $1 million to the CLAT.

---

[1] 412 disclosure: The 412(i) defined benefit pension plan is a tax-qualified retirement plan that must comply with the Employee Retirement Income Security Act of 1974, as amended (ERISA), the Internal Revenue Code of 1986, as amended, and other applicable law. For this reason, consult an attorney expert in these matters before establishing a 412(i) plan.)

Ultimately, he decided to contribute $1 million to a 15-year CLAT. Pursuant to the CLAT, the payment to charities is $35,000/year and, at the end of the term, the CLAT terminates and distributes any remaining assets to the ILIT. The beneficiaries of the ILIT are Mrs. Easton and their children.

The Result

As a result of the $1 million contribution to the CLAT, Mr. Easton obtained a current income tax deduction of $482,000 for the present value of the required charitable distributions. Since this was not a direct gift to charity but rather a "gift for the use of charity," the deductible amount was limited to 30 percent of adjusted gross income.

However, based on Mr. Easton's current year income, he was able to deduct the entire amount. The immediate $518,000 gift amount to the ILIT was offset by using up a portion of the unified credit. The client was thrilled to be able to get such a significant income tax deduction and, additionally, be able to contribute the meaningful amount to charity as a bonus. As a seasoned investor, he was equally impressed to be able to invest a significant amount on an income tax free basis, and keep all pretax earnings in excess of 3.5 percent ($35,000/$1,000,000).

In order to obtain the current income tax deduction, the CLAT needed to be of the type that requires the grantor to be taxed on all income earned by the CLAT, even though a portion of the income would be distributed to charity. In order to eliminate this tax recapture, we devised the Super CLAT investment strategy, which consisted of investing the CLAT assets into investments that do not produce any taxable income. The investment strategy consisted of tax-free municipal bonds and a variable life insurance policy insuring the client.

Because the value of the gift to the ILIT is fixed, the larger the investment return during the 15-year term of the CLAT, the better. Mr. Easton, as an investor, is convinced of his long-term ability to earn in excess of the 3.5 percent required distribution to charity. Our investment strategy was to use the $1 million to purchase municipal bonds in an amount sufficient to fund a $5 million variable universal life policy over 3 years ($255,000/year), plus the first 7 years of the charitable annuity ($35,000/year). The amounts needed for the charitable distributions during years 8–15 will be taken from the policy in the form of tax-free withdrawals.

(continued)

(continued)

Key Questions

Advisers should be asking their clients in similar situations the following questions:

- Are you aware that life insurance policies, in some cases, can be managed for even greater lifetime tax and financial advantages than for the tax and financial advantages of the death benefit?
- Are you aware how the lower cost of insurance due to longevity, investment-oriented product design and favorable tax structure have created a new diversification strategy you could call "insurance-based investing"?

Ed Wallack
Sapers & Wallack
Newton, MA

Case Study: Yesterday's Solutions, Today's Problems
Reviewing policies for suitability and performance

Key Ideas

- Policy analysis
- Nonprofit institutions
- Surrender charges

Backstory

The senior vice president (SVP) of Human Resources (HR) of a nonprofit institution, for whom I had completed projects when he was with a previous employer, called me to help evaluate insurance proposals for the institution's president.

The president was part of a 162 bonus plan for the past five years offered as a supplemental retirement program. The board of directors mandated the plan be invested in a life insurance policy.

I was told upfront that my role was only evaluation, and I would not participate in the sale of any insurance based on my findings.

The Problem

The insurance agent proposed a policy with a face value at the minimum limit (non-modified endowment contract [MEC]), given the size of the bonus. That meant that, once again, as the president's bonus increased, another life insurance policy was needed to prevent the existing policies from becoming overfunded and falling into the MEC category. For the third time in five years, an increased bonus would require a new policy and new underwriting. The president was getting annoyed and charged the SVP of HR to find the reason by comparing policies.

In the one 15-minute phone call I was given with the president, I asked him to tell me his goals of the bonus plan and the importance of the death benefit component. After all, a life insurance product can be exceptional on its own merits and still inappropriate if it doesn't achieve the insured's goals.

He was pleased to hear the question because no other agent had bothered to ask. He was strictly focused on the cash accumulation at the end of three years and was most concerned that surrender charges in the two existing policies (about three and five years old) and in the three proposed policies, would drastically reduce his bonus should his contract not be renewed at that time, or if he decided to leave voluntarily for another opportunity. He was not concerned at all with long-term performance, just the next 3 years.

(continued)

(continued)

The Decision Process

As I was asked to do, I evaluated objectively the three proposals that had been presented for the new policy—specifically regarding fees, expenses, charges, and illustrated projections based on several hypothetical, gross, and net rates of return. But none of them resolved his concerns about surrender charges.

Objectivity required exploring alternatives that would solve that issue, so I also offered a fourth proposal showing a corporate executive VUL policy, structured with term insurance, and a seven-year enhanced surrender value (honeymoon provision). This institutional product is available only in circumstances in which premium levels exceed $100,000. In this case, no one knew about this alterative, let alone that the president qualified.

With this approach, he would not only avoid surrender charges but he would receive a higher cash surrender value (CSV), the accumulation value for the first five years. In addition, his first year CSV was about 95 percent of premium.

After presenting my analysis and recommendations to the SVP of HR, he suggested I present them to the president. He was very happy with this solution and referred to it as the *wholesale alternative* because the policy fees, expenses, and charges were significantly less than the traditional *retail* policies he had previously purchased. At the end of the presentation, the president turned to the SVP of HR and, referring to our firm, said with a smile, "Why didn't you bring this firm to me before?"

The Result

We consolidated the existing policies with a total face value of $1.8 million into one for $2.75 million, allowing for a 33 percent increase in his $100,000 bonus for three consecutive years and avoiding almost any chance of needing another policy. The first year CSV (including the net transfer of approx $300,000 after surrender charges from the two existing policies) was higher than all the options from the other agents, and we lowered the internal policy costs over 40 percent.

A side benefit existed to the analysis. In comparing the fees and charges outlined in the prospectus to the policy values projected in the illustration, I noticed an error. After bringing it to the attention of the insurance company, they thanked me and sent out a correction that saved them a tremendous amount of money in potential, down-the-road problems.

Key Questions

Advisers should be asking their clients in similar situations the following:

- The advice you heard in the past may have been right, but wouldn't you like to learn whether yesterday's solutions could have become today's problems?
- Before deciding which policy to purchase, shouldn't we match the best kind of policy to the goals you want to accomplish?
- In your experience, which approach is usually better—find the cheapest solution first, or find the solution that best addresses your goals and needs first—and then look at pricing?

Ronald P. Perilstein, CLU, ChFC, CLTC
The Arjay Group, Inc.
Narberth, PA

Case Study: Small Firms Pay Big Dividends
Preparing businesses and owners for future value transitions

Key Ideas

- Role of life insurance in business transition planning
- Aligning key employee financial success with business financial success

Backstory

I was introduced to this case by a benefits broker colleague who had been working with Nordell Engineering, a 30-employee firm, for a few years and asked me to a meeting with his client about purchasing additional life insurance for protection and accumulation.

Sometimes an adviser knows there are more problems to solve but doesn't have his hand at the best pulse point, so I wasn't surprised when Andy Nordell politely declined the discussions for additional life insurance. He said he was strapped at the time due to having three children in college, and the business was in a growth mode.

I estimated he was about 50 and felt he looked a little ragged around the edges. He said the business had been operating for 25 years and confided he was actually considering ideas on how to sell the business. Life insurance was certainly not on his mind and, in fact, the broker had recommended more coverage several times in the past without a positive response.

The Problem

As our discussions continued, I learned that Andy was not thrilled at the prospect of selling the business, but he felt he couldn't continue at the pace he was running now that the business was growing. He felt there was still a lot of growth potential, but he felt resentful about all the stressful decisions that landed on his desk throughout each day.

I explained that my firm applies the SET process—succession, exit, and transition—to privately-owned firms like his. A lot of business owners at his stage of life are in the same situation. They love their business, but it has taken over their lives, and they wish there was a way to go "from overtime to part-time" while keeping the salary and benefits and their love for the business. This was exactly his concern, and he was extremely interested in hearing how that can be accomplished.

Together we identified a starting point to identify his needs and goals and explore strategies to increase the value of the business so he can get more of his life back.

The Planning Process

I led Andy through a seven-step process we developed with BEI, a consulting firm out of Denver specializing in exit planning processes for business owners. The first solution was to charge eight key employees in the firm to take more of the workload off Andy's desk and develop a plan for motivating, rewarding, and retaining this key employee group.

After evaluating several options, he settled on a phantom stock arrangement that would reward the key employees for the growth of the company's values over the next several years and provide them with a retirement benefit. The plan will also help retain the key talent by containing a rolling five-year vesting schedule on each annual "unit of value" each participant receives each year.

We funded the arrangement informally with life insurance policies that also serve as key person insurance policies on each of the key employees against the impact on the business if the employees were to die. These simple steps relieved Andy because he relied heavily on these eight employees and had always looked for ways to address the situation of providing key employee benefits.

The other motivation behind the phantom stock plan was to allow a subset of the key employees to accumulate dollars to help pay for the purchase of the business if Andy decides to sell the business to the key employees in the future. However, our planning horizon also assumed that there would not be an inside sale, but rather an outside sale, at some point in the future.

Next we addressed a deferred compensation plan for Andy that was an unfunded future liability that might limit the value of the company. Again, corporate-owned life insurance on Andy proved a more efficient way to fund the benefit and provide cost recovery.

In addition, having obtained favorable underwriting status, Andy asked me to review his personal financial situation and agreed to place another policy into an ILIT to provide for his personal estate planning.

Based on the comfort level Andy reached with the planning process, he subsequently turned over his personal assets to my firm. As his business growth accelerated, he began to harvest money from the company to reduce his reliance on the eventual sale of the company for his financial wellbeing.

(continued)

(continued)

The Result

Meanwhile, the eight key employees accepted increased responsibilities and understood that their personal financial success was now aligned with the firm's financial success. They undertook a disciplined management commitment, and Andy delegated with matching discipline. Soon, he cut a day a week out of his schedule for personal time and scheduled vacations without worrying about the firm while he traveled.

In five years, the company doubled in size, and Andy recently turned down an unsolicited offer for the firm, knowing that his business life and personal life are in balance, and that he is on solid financial ground to wait for the best offers. The family estate is in very good shape with regard to tax planning and estate planning. I meet with Andy quarterly on retainer to cover one topic per quarter that is important to him.

Key Questions

Advisers should be asking their clients in similar situations the following questions:

- What is your next goal for the business and for you personally?
- If you were going to prepare your business for sale in a few years, what has to be accomplished to maximize its value?
- Have you considered how to reward your key employees so their personal financial success is aligned with the company's financial success?
- When was the last time you revisited your estate plan in the context of future business transitions?

Bill Black, CLU, ChFC
Exit & Retirement Strategies, Inc.
Irvine, CA

Case Study: Never Too Late to Repair
Achieving legacy goals after the estate has transferred

Key Ideas

- Replacing the value of estate assets using life insurance
- Providing financial security for special needs heirs
- Preserving family privacy by avoiding probate

Backstory

I met Ramsey Kenner some years ago, and he was the wealthiest man I had ever met. His net worth was over $250 million, and he was kind enough to allow me to manage a small portion of his investment assets. I did a good job, and he introduced me to his second wife Olivia, who wanted me to manage her personal IRA of $200,000 to start.

Ramsey was considerably older than Olivia and died a few years later. Based on a prenuptial agreement, she received their home, which was also a working farm, $3 million in cash, and $5 million in a qualified terminable interest property (QTIP). She did not know until then that she did not have power to appoint assets in the QTIP, and at her death, the assets would go to his charitable endowment.

The Problem

From her perspective, it was not right that she could not appoint that $5 million to her children—two from a previous marriage. At that time, the charity was getting over $150 million. The trust gives her the greater of $250,000 of income per year or all income generated.

Now she had a $3 million farm to run with two full-time employees, and she had grown accustomed to a higher standard of living while Ramsey was alive. Her combined need for income was above the $250,000 annual income from the trust. Her remaining source of income was to draw from her $3 million investment assets. And her goal was to be able to pass the $5 million to her children.

We perceived an additional problem. After the initial estate expenses, her estate would, in fact, grow, leaving her with a tax problem of her own or a tax problem for her children after she dies. If she spends down her own assets, she would have only the farm to leave her children—an asset they would not be able to afford because the QTIP would go to the charity.

(continued)

(continued)

We then discovered that one of her children had two children to support and had fallen behind in payments. The other had personal issues, so if anything should happen to Olivia, it seemed unlikely that either of them would handle inherited assets effectively.

In addition, Ramsey's estate ended up in the newspaper because the will went through probate, and Olivia was very concerned about maintaining privacy.

The Planning Process

Replacing the $5 million was clearly the most pressing problem. Working with her attorney and CPA, we put together a simple plan to meet her lifestyle and legacy objectives and address our tax concerns. She was underwritten for a $5 million single life policy to be owned by an ILIT. Premiums were paid using gifts for three years, then upon Olivia reaching the age of 60, the policy will be paid for by distributions from an annuity we funded immediately.

The Result

We guaranteed that her children would have an inheritance of at least $5 million, free of income and estate taxes—in effect, replacing the QTIP. We also guaranteed liquidity in the event that Olivia is able to reduce her spending, and her estate increases in value. Finally, we guaranteed payment of the policy by placing money in an annuity today that will grow over four years to an amount large enough to pay the premiums for the rest of her life.

Olivia is now free of her fears about the financial future of her children. She also enjoys control over her own financial situation. And she knows her privacy will be maintained because the transfer of assets will be by beneficiary rather than by will and will not go through probate court.

Also, what her advisers have done collectively is control her spending to the tune of the $48,000 premium by forcing her to "save" that for the next 3 years. She did make her children aware of her plan and all are on board.

Key Questions

Advisers should be asking their clients in similar situations the following questions:

- Are you aware of the role life insurance can play to replace the value of illiquid estate assets for more effective asset transfer?
- Are you aware that personal information becomes public information when assets pass by will through probate court?

Brad Zapp
Legacy Financial Advisors
Covington, KY

Life Insurance Companies

6

Government Regulation of Insurance

The life insurance industry has in place a safety net of conservatism, regulation, and oversight that may not be readily apparent to the policyholders.

Although some federal laws affect life insurance, it is regulated by the states. Each state has its own set of statutes and rules. State insurance departments oversee insurer solvency, review market conduct, and rule on requests for coverage rate increases, among other responsibilities. The National Association of Insurance Commissioners (NAIC) develops model rules and regulations for the industry, many of which must be approved by state legislatures before they can be implemented.

The McCarran-Ferguson Act, passed by Congress in 1945, provides the insurance industry with a limited exemption to federal antitrust laws, allowing certain activities such as joint development of common insurance forms. The act confirms state regulation of the insurance industry as being in the public interest. However, challenges to state regulation have included proposals that advocate for a federal role in creating a more uniform system and that allow insurers the choice of a federal or state charter similar to what banks have.

Benefits of State Regulation

The fundamental reason for government regulation of insurance is to protect American consumers. The efforts of the state regulatory systems to strengthen their requirements and involvement in the industry to provide this protection have historically been successful and continue to be effective. In 1991, there were 25 life insurance company insolvencies, which was an extraordinary occurrence. Before this event, major insurance companies were always able to meet their financial obligations. But the industry's safety net held in the short term and in the long term. By 1992, 100 percent of the liabilities were recovered. 2002 showed only one insolvency.[1]

State systems are accessible and accountable to the public and are sensitive to local social and economic conditions. Insurance regulation is structured around several key functions, including company licensing, producer licensing, product regulation, market conduct, financial regulation, and consumer services.

Financial regulation provides crucial safeguards for insurance consumers. At the NAIC, the states maintain the world's largest insurance financial database, which provides a 15-year history of annual and quarterly filings on 5,200 insurance companies. Periodic financial examinations of insurance companies occur on a scheduled basis. State financial examiners investigate a company's accounting methods, procedures, and financial statement presentation. These exams verify and validate what is presented in the company's annual statement to ascertain whether the company is in good financial standing.

When an examination of financial records shows a company to be financially impaired, the state insurance department takes control of the company. Aggressively working with financially troubled companies is a critical part of the regulator's role. In the event the company must be liquidated or becomes insolvent, the states maintain a system of financial guaranty funds that cover consumers' personal losses.

Regulations to Promote Solvency

Regulations to promote solvency include minimum capital and surplus requirements, statutory accounting conventions, limits to insurance company investment and corporate activities, financial ratio tests, and financial data disclosure.

From conservative accounting rules and mandatory annual CPA audits to investment regulations and limitations, and minimum capital and surplus requirements, a state insurance regulator's toolbox allows insurers to handle greater losses than other parts of the financial sector in down-market cycles.

---

[1] See the Society of Actuaries website at www.soa.org.

Additional regulatory tools include performing ongoing financial analysis of insurers and on-site examinations. This entire solvency framework and safety net for policyholders is uniform in every state as evaluated by the NAIC Financial Regulation and Accreditation Program.

Statutory Reserves

Each insurance carrier is responsible for the liabilities associated with the life insurance policies that it sells. Carriers are required to maintain enough capital and surplus to satisfy these liabilities or obligations to policyholders. State mandated reserve calculations are based on guaranteed interest, guaranteed expenses, and guaranteed mortality assumptions.

For universal life insurance, these guaranteed assumptions create a very conservative reserve. Since the early 1990s, term and no lapse guaranteed universal life products have dominated life insurance sales. Actuarial Guidelines XXX, "Valuation of Life Insurance Policies Model Regulation," (AG XXX) and AXXX, "The Application of the Valuation of Life Insurance Policies Model Regulation," (also known as Actuarial Guideline 38 or AG AXXX) were introduced to try to address flaws in the existing statutory reserving methodology related to these two products. AG AXXX addresses reserving issues on universal life products with secondary guarantees, and these reserves are referred to as AG AXXX reserves. Generally, AG XXX addresses reserving requirements on level term products.

Even with AG XXX and AG AXXX, there is too much conservatism in the reserve calculation because the underlying mortality table has been the 1980 CSO table, and it has huge margins relative to expected mortality for certain classes of insureds. The reserves for AG XXX and AG AXXX far exceed any cash value a policy may have.

The move to the 2001 CSO table helps, but it does not recognize the benefits of modern underwriting techniques. This unnecessarily conservative approach creates a redundant reserve that requires carriers that write a lot of this business to find capital market solutions. The American Council of Life Insurers proposed the removal of some of the redundant reserve requirements to relieve some of the capital pressures carriers are facing in the current environment.

Risk Based Capital

Risk based capital (RBC) reflects the need for insurance companies to be capitalized according to the inherent riskiness of the type of insurance they sell. Higher risk types of insurance—liability as opposed to property business—generally necessitate higher levels of capital.

RBC is defined as the minimum capital and surplus that a life insurance carrier must maintain. RBC is defined in statutory laws and regulations, published and compared with a carrier's total adjusted capital. The total adjusted capital is basically the capital and surplus shown in a carrier's annual statement. Thus, RBC measures what the carrier must maintain versus what it actually has. RBC is defined in terms of the risks that a carrier assumes from

- its asset market and credit risk.
- the underwriting and pricing risk in the type of business it writes.
- disintermediation risk or the risk that the return from assets are not aligned with the requirements of the carrier's liabilities.
- general business risk.

Reinsurance

Reinsurance is insurance bought by insurers. A reinsurer assumes part of the risk and part of the premium originally taken by the insurer, known as the primary company. Reinsurance effectively increases an insurer's capital and, therefore, its capacity to sell more coverage. The business is global, and some of the largest reinsurers are based abroad. Reinsurers have their own reinsurers called "retrocessionaires." Reinsurers do not pay policyholder claims. Instead, they reimburse insurers for claims paid.

Much of the term and universal life business written in the last decade has a large percent of the mortality risk being borne by a pool of reinsurers. Each of these reinsurers has a retention amount above which they then cede to a retrocessionaire if it is a jumbo policy above the reinsurer's retention. A typical $5 million policy may have the carrier keeping $500,000, with the remaining $4.5 million being split among four to six reinsurers. This provides an extra amount of diversification. In 2006, as much as 60 percent of new business was ceded to reinsurers. In 2007, it was about 40 percent.

Reinsurance not only provides mortality protection for carriers, it also offers carriers capital management solutions. Reinsurers have functioned as an aggregator of redundant reserves for their carrier clients and have employed capital market solutions to help smaller carriers get statutory reserve relief. Reinsurers have a reputation for being strongly capitalized.

Insolvency

In its simplest form, *insolvency* refers to an insurance company's inability to pay the claims of policyholders. Insurance insolvency standards, and the regulatory actions taken, vary from state to state.

When regulators deem an insurance company is in danger of becoming insolvent, they can take one of three actions: place a company in conservatorship or rehabilitation if the company can be saved, or place a company in liquidation if salvage is deemed impossible. The difference between the first two options is one of degree; regulators guide companies in conservatorship but direct those in rehabilitation.

Typically, the first sign of problems is an insurer's inability to pass the financial tests regulators administer as a routine procedure.

The following are actions state insurance regulators can take to prevent an insurer from failing.

Conservation

Conservation is when the insurance regulator takes over the operations of an insurance company to conserve assets for the benefit of policyholders, creditors, and other persons interested in the assets of the company. One of the regulator's main duties is to conduct a thorough examination of the insurance company's books and records to determine whether the company can be rehabilitated.

Rehabilitation

Rehabilitation generally involves the regulator initiating a plan to return the company to a sound financial and operational condition. If efforts are not successful, then the state would place the insurer in liquidation.

Liquidation

The *liquidation* process ordinarily includes the seizure, marshalling, and liquidation of a company's assets and distribution of those assets to claimants with approved claims.

If assets are not adequate to fully satisfy approved claims, the guaranty associations provide additional claims payments up to specific state coverage and limitation statutes, similar to Federal Deposit Insurance Corporation (FDIC) coverage for bank accounts.

Insurance company liquidations are subject to each state's liquidation statutes and not the Federal Bankruptcy Code. An order of liquidation enables the state insurance department, or its appointed deputy, to wind up the insurance company's affairs by selling its assets and settling claims upon those assets.

In practice, when an insurance company becomes insolvent, other life insurance companies that are headquartered or do business in the same state will rescue the faltering company. This is recognized as one of the responsibilities of companies that do business in that state. The state's life companies can be assessed by the state regulators to help with the bailout, but frequently—especially if it is a small company that is in trouble—a larger company will take it over on its own initiative or with only the slightest encouragement by the regulator.

The policyholders of the failed company may be unable to withdraw money from their policies for some time, but eventually, they will probably get all, or nearly all, of what they are entitled to under their contracts.

Policyholder Protection

Protection can be provided in one of several different ways. For example, a financially sound insurer may take over the troubled company's policies and assume the responsibility for continuing coverage and paying covered claims.

Claims from individual policyholders are given the utmost priority over other creditors in these matters. And, in the unlikely event that assets are not enough to cover these claims, another safety net is in place to protect consumers: state guaranty funds. These funds are in place in all states. If an insurance company becomes unable to pay claims, the guaranty fund will provide coverage, subject to certain limits—again, similar to the FDIC's coverage for bank accounts.

The State Guaranty Fund

The state guaranty fund is a mechanism by which solvent insurers ensure that some of the policyholder and third-party claims against failed insurance companies are paid. State guaranty funds are supported by assessments on insurers doing business in the state. State guaranty funds are required in all 50 states, the District of Columbia, and Puerto Rico.

However, the type and amount of claim covered by the fund varies by state. For example, some states pay policyholders unearned premiums, which is the portion of the premium for which no coverage was provided because the company was insolvent. A complete list of guaranty fund coverage by state is available at the National Organization of Life and Health Insurance Guaranty Associations.[2]

The state guaranty association may provide coverage directly by continuing the insurer's policies or issuing replacement policies with the guaranty association. In some situations, the association may work with other state guaranty associations to develop an overall plan to provide protection for the failed insurer's policyholders. The amount of protection provided, and when a policyholder receives it, may depend on the particular arrangement worked out for handling the failed insurer's policyholder obligations.

Ratings

Several major credit agencies determine the financial strength and viability of an insurer to meet claims obligations. They include the following:

- A.M. Best Co.
- Fitch, Inc.
- Moody's Investors Services
- Standard & Poor's Corp
- Weiss Ratings, Inc.
- Comdex[3]

---

[2] See The National Organization of Life and Health Insurance Guaranty Associations online at www.nolhga.com.

[3] Comdex is not a rating agency; it is a composite of all the ratings that a company has received.

Factors these agencies consider include company earnings; capital adequacy; operating leverage; liquidity; investment performance; reinsurance programs; and management ability, integrity, and experience.

Life insurance consists of promises the policyholder makes to an insurance company (primarily to pay premiums) and promises the insurance company makes to the policyholder (mostly to pay the claim). Life insurance company ratings are one measure of the extent to which policyholders can rely on a company to live up to those promises. If the company is financially sound, it is highly likely to be able to pay the death claim or the cash surrender value when required. If the company has a very high rating, it will usually have no difficulty at all in fulfilling its contractual obligations.

Low-rated companies can be more problematic, but most low-rated companies are able to pay their claims. Of the 3,000 or so life insurance companies, only a very few get in really serious financial trouble. Even the ones that cannot pay their claims are eventually rescued by the insurance regulators and other insurers.

Distinctions Among Share Price, Ratings, and Solvency

Share price is a significant indicator of earnings for financial markets and insurers' ratings from credit agencies. However, a declining share price does not mean that a policyholder's coverage has suddenly deteriorated or that an insurer is no longer solvent and unable to pay claims. In short, rating downgrades and drops in share price do not change an insurer's ability to pay claims.

Parent Company

A noninsurance parent company is federally regulated and, therefore, not held to the same investment, accounting, and capital adequacy standards as its state-regulated insurance subsidiaries. In most cases, the insurance subsidiaries are solvent and able to pay their obligations. Interestingly, it will likely be the insurance subsidiaries—or their valuable blocks of business and high-quality assets—that will be sold in an attempt to return the noninsurance parent company to a stable financial position.

Life insurance subsidiaries of a noninsurance holding company, or parent company, are separate and distinct legal entities. Although the subsidiaries are part of the parent, each insurance company subsidiary of the parent is responsible for the obligations associated with its contracts.

For example, in the case of American International Group, Inc. (AIG), conventional wisdom dictates that the AIG insurer subsidiaries' assets are beyond the direct reach of AIG creditors. State and federal law requires insurers to be rehabilitated or liquidated in state courts under statutory schemes roughly analogous to federal bankruptcy law. Insurance commissioners and superintendents have broad power to block sales of insurance company assets and wholesale movement of insurance company capital. As a result, under the conventional wisdom, the wide arm of state regulation would surround AIG subsidiaries in the event of AIG insolvency.

Because insurance subsidiaries are regulated by states, they are not subject to the federal laws that would affect their noninsurance holding company parent, should it seek bankruptcy protection. When an insurance holding company declares bankruptcy, one of the state regulators' concerns is whether the parent will try to go after the insurance subsidiaries' assets to satisfy creditors.

As a result, state regulators could intervene and place the insurance subsidiaries into receivership, not because they are insolvent, but because of the need to protect the assets of the insurance subsidiaries.

Another risk the insurance subsidiaries face if the parent company files for bankruptcy is potential ratings downgrades. Technically, the parent is a totally different financial enterprise from the insurance subsidiary so the financial ratings should not be the same. However, the fear factor regarding the parent may have an effect on its insurance subsidiaries.

Assets in a Separate Account

A *separate account* generally refers to an investment account maintained separately from an insurer's general account to manage the funds placed in variable insurance products such as variable universal life or variable annuities. In fact, state insurance law requires insurance company separate accounts to be held apart from the rest of the company assets.

Therefore, the separate account assets are held for the exclusive benefit of the clients and their beneficiaries.

This ensures that the account is not subject to claims from any person or entity other than a contract owner, plan participant, or beneficiary. This is in distinct contrast to the insurer's *general account*, an undivided investment account in which insurers maintain funds that support contractual obligations for guaranteed insurance products, such as whole life insurance or fixed-rate annuities.

One benefit to the consumer is separate accounts are generally not chargeable with liabilities arising out of any other business the insurance company may conduct. As a result, a separate account offers policyholders some measure of protection against carrier insolvency unavailable with traditional products. However, the carrier must be able to pay the death benefit in excess of the cash value, so its ability to meet that obligation is a policyholder's legitimate concern.

Mutual Versus Stock

A *mutual life insurance company* is a life insurance provider that is owned by its policyholders. Unlike a mutual life insurance company, a *stock life insurance company* is owned by its shareholders and is publicly traded. As a result, stock companies face intense pressure from their shareholders to perform. Stock companies pay close attention to daily fluctuations in stock price. As stock prices slip during tough economic times, shareholders place extreme pressure on a stock company to improve results and increase the stock price.

In contrast, mutual companies are not publicly traded, do not answer to shareholders, and are not scrutinized in the same fashion as a stock company. Simply put, a mutual company does not have to satisfy the demands of shareholders. With a mutual company, no inherent conflict of interest exists between shareholders and policyholders. Mutual companies can take a long-term approach because they do not have to pay attention to daily fluctuations in stock prices. As a result, products offered by mutual companies during tough economic times can achieve a lower return on investment without facing scrutiny from shareholders. Apart from its ownership structure, a mutual life insurance company functions quite similarly to other insurance companies.

Stock and mutual offer comparable forms of life insurance, including term, whole life, adjustable, and other indemnity contracts, and ultimately share a similar mission: global competition across multiple product lines.

Products issued by stock and mutual companies are subject to the same scrutiny by state regulators with regard to solvency, including minimum capital and surplus requirements, statutory accounting conventions, limits to insurance company investment and corporate activities, financial ratio tests, and financial data disclosure.

Prior to liquidation, when one carrier acquires another carrier, the acquiring carrier is required to meet the contractual obligations of the selling carrier. Certain types of contracts contain obligations that are guaranteed, such as no-lapse guarantee products with guaranteed premiums, guaranteed interest crediting rates, and charges. The acquiring carrier must honor these guarantees and cannot alter the guarantees provided under the terms of the original contract. With regard to nonguaranteed provisions of the contract, the acquiring carrier could alter these terms by decreasing crediting rates or increasing charges, which may adversely affect the contract values.

Life Insurance Professionals 7

When professional advisers work successfully together, tacit understanding of and sensitivity to the *rules* of client relationships exists. It is not because they have the best *intentions*, rather they demonstrate to each other their skill in communicating and building trust with clients. Competence, capabilities, and long-term commitment mean nothing without the shared assurance that they both sit on the client's side of the table.

Independence

A critical factor to sitting on the client's side of the table that professional advisers expect from their counterparts in the life insurance industry is independence. The assumption is that insurance professionals who can only represent one company cannot provide clients with enough options to assure the best decision.

But just having relationships with a large number of companies isn't a good measure of independence because life insurance decisions in the advanced markets are not a simple bidding process. Having influence with companies can bring advantages and concession to your clients, and influence doesn't spread consistently over a large number of companies.

Decades ago, captive agents of large insurance companies existed— those with a huge investment in recruiting, training, and supporting their distribution system. And there were so-called "independent brokers," who dealt with many smaller companies—who kept their investment in distribution to a minimum. Each kind of agent brought something of value to the table, but neither really sat on the client's side. The captive agent, by definition, represented the company. The independent agent had little clout with any company.

It was the top agents in the captive arena who broke out and changed the nature of life insurance distribution in the client's favor by giving independence a new meaning.

These agents had established themselves in the top of the market—the advanced applications of life insurance for affluent families and corporations—and realized that their companies' products and resources were necessarily geared down to the middle of the market, where volume was more valuable than client quality.

Most of them tried for years to persuade or finesse management to provide them the dedicated resources they were convinced, rightfully, they had earned. However for most, the results were so frustrating that they contemplated what was completely taboo—leaving their companies whose products they previously had sold exclusively, giving up the market position the former carrier's name provided, and very importantly going on the hook personally for all the resources they needed. It wasn't just a few of the top producers in the top companies who took this path. Once a handful succeeded, a wave followed.

With the wave came enlightenment—they saw how much they had in common with their colleagues around the country who had taken the same leap into independence. They joined forces to negotiate with selected life insurance companies for access to better products for their affluent and corporate niches. They shared the investment in the technology to replace and upgrade what their companies had provided. They shared ideas about how to successfully use independence to position themselves not as the best salespeople, but as trusted insurance advisers.

Within a few years, the network of relationships evolved into distribution companies. Soon these distribution companies had enough critical mass to negotiate on an institution-to-institution basis with product and service providers. They negotiated on behalf of their target market, turning the agency model into an independent distribution company model, more often than not, with the very life insurance companies who resisted their demands when they were their top captive agents.

This is the ideal representation of independence:

- The most knowledgeable and experienced minds in the industry sharing their expertise and creativity for the good of the target market
- Purchasing power to leverage product development and technology development to the target market

- Proprietary design, administration, and communication systems tied to insurance company financial data and management systems on behalf of the target market

However, independence is worth very little, if the insurance professional can't do the job. So professional advisers need to know how to test expertise, experience, and resources and match their clients' needs to the right capabilities.

Professional Designations

One proof of expertise is the right professional designation and professional associations. The most common professional designation indicating in-depth knowledge of life insurance and its applications is the chartered life underwriter (CLU). A chartered financial consultant (ChFC) has additional personal financial planning background.

Membership in the Association of Advanced Life Underwriters (AALU) also should indicate a dedication to state-of-the-art planning techniques and current legislative and regulatory issues. Membership in your area's Estate Planning Council indicates a commitment to continuing education in all aspects of family wealth transfer. At the national level, the National Association of Estate Planners and Councils offers the Accredited Estate Planner (AEP) designation.

Sharing Information

One way to test client resources and a commitment to keeping clients informed is the frequency and sophistication level of educational communications sent by the insurance professional's firm—newsletters, tax advisories, financial and economic news, and so forth. Of course, an underlying marketing motive exists, but creating informed clients and professional advisers is a highly principled marketing strategy.

Another measure of resources is the degree to which support staff assist clients directly because they know the answers, have been given authority to handle selected problems, and take responsibility for their responses. This initiative should indicate the insurance professional has made an effort to pass along his or her knowledge in order to enhance client service. On the other hand, financial services regulatory agencies set very stringent licensing requirements and very specific communication standards, so an insurance professional whose staff exceeds these limits should raise red flags.

Sales Approach

Decades ago, life insurance products were seldom marketed as anything but variations on a basic risk management tool. Selling life insurance did not require sophisticated planning expertise, and agents were trained more on getting clients to buy than finding ways to solve their problems. This old school approach is still around, and clients tend to immediately hate it.

Distinguishing between insurance professionals and insurance salespeople is relatively simple if you pay attention to their approach. Salespeople focus on product features and benefits very early. Insurance professionals take a consultative approach, asking questions, and listen to answers in order to appreciate the nuances of client problems and tailor the most effective solutions. They view their role as advocates for clients, implying a standard of helping clients make their own informed decisions.

Disclosure

Many insurance professionals have broken with tradition and have no hesitation about openly disclosing commission structures of products or consulting fee. Professional advisers should develop an understanding with the insurance professional in advance about appropriate commission structures for particular products, carriers, and services.

Relationships

Professional advisers should ask for a list of CPAs and attorneys with whom an insurance adviser and his or her staff works regularly, and they should contact those referral sources for their views on the working relationship and the perceived value to clients.

The A-Team

Independence and the right capabilities count for a lot, but not enough to trump a less-than-satisfying working relationship. Insurance decisions for business owners, corporations, and affluent families are not made in isolation. Several disciplines must come together to integrate financial options, tax effects, and personal and business issues. Not to mention, the implementation and ongoing administrative resources that the decisions set in motion should be incorporated.

In such a planning environment, merging advisers into a team is the only reasonable approach. What does it take to maintain the team?

Knowledge of Respective Disciplines

Every advisory field (legal, accounting, investment, insurance, banking, and trusts) has become so complicated, each profession has enough to do to gain in-depth knowledge just in their own focus area. All professional advisers often have stacks of articles to study from their own field, and they all have continuing education commitments to meet every year.

A successful team approach requires even more. Advisers must get outside their own narrow view so that they can serve their client with both precise expertise and broadening vision. They must drop their biases, put aside their egos, and recognize the magnitude of every team member's contribution to the client's welfare.

Conflicting Interests

When sophisticated clients pay for high-level advice, they want to know clearly for what they are paying and what it buys. They need some security that their interests come first, and that compensation is earned by advocating those interests.

One downside to the team approach is the various ways in which advisers are compensated for their contribution to the decision-making process. One profession works on project fees, another on a combination of fees and contingencies, another on periodic management fees, another on asset-based fees, and still another on commissions. And all of them can compensate each other by mutual referrals and expansion of influence.

All these compensation structures have openings for conflicts of interest, real or perceived. They must be acknowledged upfront. The client can never be the last to know or the whole team structure, and all the value it offers the client, comes into question.

Responsibilities and Procedures

Default standards should be established as an informal contract agreed to by the team for its working relationship—authority, assignments, time-frames, and lines of communication among the team and to the client. The client may add, delete, or amend the defaults. A written standard is the closest thing to a guarantee that expectations are realistic and serves as a form of proof of their having been met.

The implementation plan provides the signposts for the client to measure progress toward his or her goals. Airplanes don't take off without flight plans and checklists. Epic movies are not made without a script, a storyboard, and a production schedule that organizes a sequencing of shots, location by location, for the most cost effective use of resources. In warfare, logistics saves more lives than courage. Even when the team's working relationship has a good history, only the present means anything to the client.

When advisers work alone, they can get away with manageable uncertainty and drift. But a team will flounder without precise operational control. The client wonders why with all this talent so little happens the way it was expected.

Advance Sign-off

Insurance planning for business owners, corporations, and affluent families requires a substantial amount of goal-setting and customization. There are as many soft issues as hard ones to resolve, and as many emotions in the equation as numbers.

It is an art to detect the nuances in all the data and with several pairs of sophisticated ears at work, every likelihood exists that conclusions will vary from adviser to adviser. For that reason, consensus on client objectives and solution specifications is critical. Without it, down the line someone will find flaws where others saw ingenuity. What the client will see is justification for doubts—or worse.

Documentation

Not only is sign-off to the plan by all parties necessary at the conceptual stage, it becomes even more important at the incremental decision stages. Decision patterns of this complexity are difficult to reconstruct when months and years have passed, but not if everyone's files (adviser's and client's) reflect the same history.

Review and Modification

When the plan has become operational, each adviser will have his or her own tasks to perform and his or her own perspective on the ongoing administration, reporting, and service needs. Because the focus changes from the client to the task, a tendency for communication standards to loosen among the team members exists.

Although the tasks of design and implementation may have ended, the plan itself never ends. Ideally, periodic review procedures should bring the team back together.

But even when this is impractical or unwarranted, the reporting of future decisions cannot be ignored. The breakdown of the team approach to solving client problems is reached when one team member asks, "Why wasn't I informed of this?" It is the thin end of the wedge for future problems.

Case Study: New Value From Old Policies
Refinancing strategies for life insurance

Key Ideas

- Policy review
- Policy structure and ownership strategies
- Premium funding strategies
- Irrevocable life insurance trust

Backstory

Over several years, our firm has enjoyed a strategic partnership with Marc Parkinson, managing partner of Petrinovich, Pugh & Co. He is the past chairman of the California Society of Certified Public Accountants and council member of the AICPA.

The impact of this strategic partnership is teaming with Petrinovich, Pugh & Co. to assist clients with any financial planning, insurance, and accounting needs they may have. The process includes weekly meetings to update each other on our work for respective clients and keep both firms 100 percent involved in the entire client decision process.

In 2007, Marc discovered through his annual review procedures that a comprehensive insurance evaluation for the Goddard family had not been undertaken in a long time. He asked Stan Goddard to approve a review of coverage by our firm in order to analyze policy performance and suitability and to make recommendations to improve the value of the life insurance component of their portfolio.

The Problem

We learned from Marc that Stan and Kate Goddard had a net worth in the $100 million range, the majority of it in real estate, by means of partnerships, limited liability companies (LLCs), and other fractionalized ownership structures. Roughly 30 percent was in cash, and they wanted to increase their cash position to $50 million over the next 3–5 years.

Stan is in his late 60s, Kate is younger, and although they have three unmarried children, Eric (28), Amy (23), and Laurie (21), no wealth transfer strategies—current or long-range—had been planned, let alone initiated.

Nevertheless, guaranteeing that his children receive the inheritance he had mentally set aside for them was a priority. He was concerned that if he "lost it all," then the children would lose their inheritance. Because the tax structure of life insurance provides a more efficient way to resolve that concern, we added this issue to our evaluation of their life insurance portfolio.

The evaluation revealed that by using the cash value in their current policies while maintaining the same ongoing premium cost, the Goddards could have two to three times their current death benefit. It wasn't that their existing policies were poor decisions, but with mortality rates going down and the improved guarantees available on new products, the current policies were no longer efficient vehicles, considering the ongoing premiums that Stan was paying. In addition, because the $9 million in death benefits were structured to pass to the children as part of the estate, the net benefit would be reduced by estate tax to only $5 million.

Marc told us Stan had been approached in the past by insurance agents offering to increase the death benefit for the existing premium amount, and he had not been interested. He was concerned that he would be paying for additional coverage that would not be fully guaranteed and wasn't interested in surprises down the road. Stan also has a close relationship with his current insurance agent, now semiretired, and he was skeptical about using someone new. However, he realized there was some risk that his agent had not remained current on all the recent changes to life insurance structure and pricing.

At Marc's request, we sent Stan a one-page executive summary explaining what my company, Legacy, could potentially do for them beyond simply increasing the coverage by replacing old policies.

First the summary showed that their $100 million net worth is subject to $45 million in estate taxes. Although life insurance is generally the most efficient way to fund estate taxes, the current policies, subject to estate taxes, will fund only $5 million. So Stan's concern about the unlikely possibility of "losing it all" was dwarfed by the certainty that the government would take all the family's $30 million of cash assets and the $5 million life insurance benefit, leaving their three children owing $10 million of their inheritance to the IRS—with no funding and a potentially distressed sale of their inherited assets.

(continued)

(continued)

The Solution

Then our executive summary showed Stan that he could dramatically increase the death benefit to an estimated $26 million, guaranteed and not subject to estate tax, without increasing premium. The new math now looked like this:

- $100 million estate—$30 million cash and $70 million illiquid
- $45 million estate tax liability
- $26 million life insurance benefit to fund liability
- $19 million cash assets to fund balance of tax liability
- $11 million of cash assets saved making new estate value $81 million
- $0 estate tax shortfall
- $0 added premium expense

Based on that summary, the Goddards asked Marc to begin the planning process with Legacy Capital Group. However, as we probed deeper into the circumstances, a few more issues emerged that needed to be resolved:

- Some of the policies could not be surrendered because there was about $650,000 of gain in those policies, which would subject them to income tax. We accomplished a 1035 exchange on two of the most profitable policies on Kate's life. This eliminated $450,000 of the total $650,000 gain, leaving only a $200,000 gain.
- For the purpose of estate tax strategies, the wrong type of policies had been purchased. Individual life policies that provided wealth replacement for Kate needed to be restructured as joint-and-survivor policies to pay estate taxes.
- In addition, three different entities owned policies in the portfolio—individuals, property trusts, and an insurance trust with incorrect trustees and administration provisions. Legacy and Marc recommended a local attorney to rectify the legal issues with the trusts because the lawyer the Goddards used previously was not actively managing their trusts, and the relationship was not close. All the policies are now trust owned by an irrevocable life insurance trust (ILIT).
- Because the current annual premiums of $125,000 were our benchmark for increasing coverage at no added cost, and because the Goddards' annual gift tax exclusion limit is $48,000, we need to design a plan to pay the same premium amount on the new policies without triggering a gift tax. This was accomplished by transferring units of a real estate investment structured as

an LLC that happens to produce a lot of cash flow into the ILIT. Using the tax advantages of the LLC structure and the grantor trust status of the ILIT, along with the Goddards' lifetime exemptions and their annual gift tax exclusions, all premiums for the restructured life insurance portfolio are covered in the most efficient manner.

- Finally, when we submitted applications for underwriting bids, some medical issues were raised that affected Stan and Kate's underwriting classification. Because these issues came from decades ago, and the entire Goddard family are avid healthy living enthusiasts, we engaged our underwriting advocate resources at NFP to negotiate with NFP's core insurance companies on the Goddards' behalf. When the facts were reexamined, they both received preferred ratings.

The Result

With the help of case design specialists from NFP's Large Case Unit, the Goddards had a coordinated team come up with a well-structured plan that resolved virtually all of the issues that arose during the decision process. We also included the Goddards' current semiretired agent in the decision, and he agreed that these were good solutions for the client.

Because this planning process required a significant shift in mindset for the Goddards in a number of areas—new perspectives on life insurance, wealth transfer, outside advisers, and so forth—to make them comfortable, we met with them and Marc every two weeks to review progress and lay out the next steps in a clear and comprehensible PowerPoint presentation.

The Goddards were very pleased to find peace of mind that their children's inheritance is safe and secure, and a great business—as well as personal relationship—quickly evolved. We will be exploring additional wealth accumulation and wealth transfer strategies to even further enhance the Goddards' legacy.

Marc Parkinson was also pleased with the entire process. Afterwards he reported, "As a CPA, your normal mode is taking care of routine business for your client, which doesn't provide much opportunity to innovate. When you can add value for your client, it is very satisfying. This innovative solution tripled my client's insurance protection and removed the death benefit from the estate, saving millions of dollars in estate taxes."

(continued)

(continued)

We learned in our debriefing that he felt well-informed and able to discuss the case with his client knowledgeably throughout the process. He could see early on that he could not have done this on his own, so the value of partnering with a firm that has the expertise for a complicated case and can execute from start to finish cannot be overestimated.

Key Questions

Advisers should be asking their clients in similar situations the following questions:

- When was the last time your agent completed an audit of your life insurance policies to see if it's time to refinance and capture more capital value?
- Do you know if your policies' costs are fully guaranteed, or can the cost go up?
- Do you have coverage that you no longer need or feel that you can't afford?
- Were multiple companies considered when you purchased your policy, or was one company only recommended by your insurance adviser?

Richard Baer
Legacy Capital Group California
Los Gatos, CA

Marc Parkinson, CPA
Petrinovich, Pugh & Co.
San Jose, CA

Case Study: Dreams in the Back of a Client's Mind
The right order for planning is goals first, numbers second

Key Idea

- Charitable planning for lifetime and legacy

Background

A good friend and strategic alliance partner was asked by a client, the Careys, for advice about a life insurance decision they were considering. They had a net worth over $50 million from a successful business in the financial services arena. Their current planning included several irrevocable trusts that have been, and will be, gifted assets over time, and Victor Carey had applied his financial experience to select the investments in the trusts.

However, he was not equally familiar with life insurance, though he recognized distinct income tax advantages that could benefit the trusts. He wanted an outsider with more depth of life insurance knowledge to evaluate the suitability and projected performance of the policies he had been shown and to confirm the advantages before making his decision. Our friend put him in touch with our firm.

They had been shown a survivorship policy illustration with a $20 million death benefit and were told that it was a product not available to the general public. Their understanding was that a single premium of $1.2 million would support the death benefit forever.

The Problem

Our analysis raised doubts. First, the product was not in any way proprietary, and was, in fact, a regular shelf product available to the general public. Second, the single premium supported the death benefit for only 10 years, not forever, as they understood. In the eleventh year, a second lump sum premium was shown in the illustration. This second premium came from a grantor retained annuity trust (GRAT), and we believed it assumed an unrealistically high return on investment, given the cash flow requirements.

Victor agreed with our findings once he saw more clearly how to evaluate the illustration. He was convinced that we knew what we were talking about, and he decided to meet with us again to consider his alternatives. We explained how alternatives should be based on their goals first, then on all the relevant facts of

(continued)

(continued)

their current financial situation, including trust and estate documents. We needed to discuss goals in depth; however, we offered to show conceptual alternatives as a starting point. He agreed and also expressed an interest in term insurance in order to buy time for his investment strategies to bear fruit.

The Solution

At the second meeting, we diagramed the broad elements of the current estate plan for Victor and his wife Susan, pointing out that the $20 million estate tax at the second death was based on the estate values today and needed to address future growth. The insurance concept we presented was private placement variable survivorship universal life with maximum funding and an endorsement of the net amount at risk (NAR) to an ILIT. The funding amount resulted in a NAR that was approximately the $20 million for the first 10 years, then diminishing over the next 10 years. We also discussed term insurance premiums.

Ben did not feel comfortable with the private placement concept because he believed the hedge fund marketplace had become commoditized and would not be producing the level of returns it has in the past. He also felt that he had enough exposure to that investment type through his own work and did not want to allocate any additional assets.

Then, as the meeting was ending, he opened up the real planning goal he had in the back of his mind. He wanted to build sufficient assets in the trusts to allow him to leave the taxable estate to charity. He repeated that he liked the idea of term insurance because it would buy time for this to take place. None of the information we received from them and through his estate planning attorneys indicated this was a goal, but with it we could begin to move from conceptual to actual.

The Results

We met again and presented a maximum funded variable life policy owned by one of the existing trusts, paid for with existing trust assets. The NAR of the policy was approximately equal to what the heirs would receive under the current estate plan. We suggested that this policy served two main purposes:

- It allowed the Careys to amend their estate plan by leaving their assets to charity now, rather than in the future.
- It created a tax efficient asset for the trust in the future when Victor "switched off" the grantor trust status and the trust needed to pay its own income taxes.

He saw that he did not need to "buy time," and the idea was immediately well received. From there he approved all the related elements of the planning process to move forward. When the policy was issued, Victor and Susan met with their estate planning attorney to redraft their planning documents to create and fund a family foundation at their death.

Although our involvement started as a second opinion, our focus on goals ahead of financial analysis brought a thought process out of the client he had not even revealed to his advisers. He thought he had to put everything in place first and then create a plan. Without hearing that dream, we could not have helped him make a sound financial decision today. He would have missed the opportunity to make equally sound financial decisions that actually set in motion his future dream today.

Key Questions

Advisers should be asking their clients in similar situations the following questions:

- When you take a long-term view of the wealth you have successfully achieved so far, what is in the back of your mind about the best way to use it?
- Is your team of advisers aware of that dream?
- How effectively does your current estate plan support that dream?
- To make sure you won't lose the value of family capital inside a life insurance policy you no longer need, shouldn't you have the policy evaluated by an expert who can present you with alternatives?
- To make sure you are receiving the most effective solutions, shouldn't you be considering only creative, customized, hand-crafted alternatives?
- To make sure you are receiving the most efficient life insurance pricing possible, shouldn't you have medical experts negotiating on your behalf?

Jordon Katz
JR Katz
Northbrook, IL

Case Study: Split Dollar Traps
Protecting clients today from past decisions gone wrong

Key Ideas

- Importance of policy review
- Split dollar compliance strategies

Backstory

One of my best clients is also one of my most challenging clients—a very successful entrepreneur who thrives on instinct, intuition, and positive thinking and seldom looks back.

I became the broker of record for his company's qualified retirement plan, nonqualified deferred compensation plan, and other company benefits. In addition, he asked me to help him develop a family wealth mission statement that put his tax, financial, and legacy philosophies on paper and organized his estate assets for planning purposes.

The Problem

In completing that project, I discovered he had purchased from a previous insurance adviser $40 million of life insurance coverage on a collateral assignment split dollar basis. But what concerned me was that there were no split dollar agreements or collateral assignment agreements to be found.

As we all know, the IRS had been questioning split dollar purchases of life insurance from a tax perspective for several years. Finally, the IRS effectively pulled the rug out from under the advantages of split dollar arrangements with new regulations with which my free spirit entrepreneurial client would have to comply.

I knew the concept of compliance was not going to inspire him, so I immediately asked to audit those policies. It was difficult to convince him that he had a problem, not to mention conveying the magnitude of the problem. He didn't realize that his previous agent had not completed the job, ignored critical documentation, and failed to inform my clients' other planning advisers.

He had $40 million of second-to-die insurance arranged in 8 different policies, purchased separately over an 8-year period. All of them were collateral assignment split dollar, and I found 1 agreement with the first policy dated 16 years ago that was assumed to cover all 8. None of them was structured with any rollout strategy other than the possible rollout at the first death of the husband insured.

No assets had ever been booked on the corporate balance sheet, and no annual U.S. Life Table 38 values had been reported to the insureds and trustees of the policy owner—an ILIT, for either income or gift tax purposes. My client had already used his and his wife's lifetime gift tax exemptions to fund other family planning gifts of company stock and wanted to continue to use their annual gift tax exclusions to gift company stock. This was obviously problematic to accommodate annual and lifetime gift tax issues.

The annual premium flow to support all of this was in excess of $240,000, increasing the ultimate split dollar rollout to an insurmountable number. In addition, the ILIT owned stock from Prudential & Manulife from their earlier demutualization, totaling $550,000.

Knowing the new split dollar regulations, accounting requirements, and taxation, I needed to give him the strategic plan for unraveling his second-to-die split dollar life insurance arrangement before the IRS unraveled it for him with a huge income tax hit.

The Solution

I laid out my recommendations as follows:

- You need to stop paying premiums and establish another formal way of paying premiums.
- We need to determine whether the existing policies are worth keeping— assuming we can determine the right method to finance the annual premiums or whether new insurance could be financed more efficiently.
- We need to bring in your accounting firm to calculate the correct balance sheet structure to the split dollar plan, book it on the balance sheets of the company, and begin properly accounting for the annual U.S. Life Table 38 income and gift tax purposes.
- With your adviser team, you need to review the new "Loan Regime" and "Economic Benefit Regime" to determine the future accounting of any policies that may remain in split dollar when all the dust settles.
- We need to determine an ultimate rollout and repayment strategy for the split dollar plan.

The Results

With his advisory team, he created an installment sale to a defective trust (IDIT) of the real estate that houses the family business. The resulting positive cash

(continued)

(continued)

flow from the real estate rental income to the trusts—for the benefit of the ILIT beneficiaries—will begin to provide cash flow to pay the annual premiums needed without funding from the corporation.

Three of the original policies were kept in split dollar—two structured in a loan regime, the third in the economic benefit regime. Premium payments were no longer needed in all three policies and are offset with policy dividends or cash value interest. This left the total face amount in split dollar of $21 million.

The other policies were surrendered (total face amount of $19 million), and cash values were applied to pay back the split dollar advances. The Prudential and Manulife stock was also liquidated to help facilitate the repayment of the split dollar advances.

The ILIT then purchased new "no lapse guaranteed adjustable life" policies, financed with the cash from the Prudential and Manulife stock sales as well as cash flow from the IDIT. The new coverage totaled $20 million. These steps eliminated all premium payments by the corporation and all further split dollar advances. As a result, the total cash flow needed for life insurance went from $240,000 to $110,000.

Most important, my client's life insurance plan was in compliance, his advisers were informed, documentation was in order, and no traps or surprises lie ahead.

Key Questions

Advisers should be asking their clients in similar situations the following questions:

- How long has it been since your life insurance policies were reviewed by an expert to measure their performance and validate their suitability for your current goals?
- Do you have any life insurance policies with split dollar financing arrangements, and are they in compliance with the latest regulations?
- Do you have a family wealth mission statement that sets forth your tax, financial, and legacy philosophies and your goals for family wealth over generations?

Mark Winter
EBA Insurance & Financial Services
Thousand Oaks, CA

Case Study: I Thought All I Wanted Was a Shower
The importance of discovery in collaborative planning

Key Ideas

- Adviser collaboration
- Comprehensive planning

Background

A few years ago, I bought a 50-year-old home in a great area, knowing at some point I would make substantial additions, upgrades, and changes. Before I reached the stage of actually developing the plan for the remodel, I noticed mold growing in the master bathroom shower.

As long as I had to repair the problem, I thought I would lead off the remodel with a magnificent double shower—stone, glass, multiple fixtures, steam. I selected a general contractor who finished the job in a month. Except—now my masterpiece shower stood completely inappropriately in a very old-fashioned bathroom. As long as I had the shower, I decided to remodel the bathroom entirely.

That was the beginning of a long downward spiral in which every new idea seemed to begin with the phrase, "As long as ....":

- As long as I was remodeling the bathroom, I should draw up preliminary plans for the entire reconstruction process.
- As long as I was going to change the roofline, I should raise the ceilings to match contemporary styling.
- But to raise the ceilings, I would need stronger studs.
- And to support the larger studs I would need a new foundation.
- A new foundation meant tearing the house to the ground—all but my shower!

With so many decisions to make each day, I put off all the details of finishes, flooring, hardware, and so forth, reasoning that those choices would become clearer as the project progressed. But I learned that every choice became an expensive change order—90 change orders in all!

Of course, I got no decision advice from any of the contractors. They simply waited for me, content to let me make my mistakes and pay them higher fees as the punishment I deserved.

(continued)

(continued)

The Problem

In the estate planning world, the same thing can happen to clients if we let it happen. Most successful business owners we work with have already taken some steps to create, protect, and preserve their business and family assets. Prodded by their attorneys, accountants, and insurance advisers, who can see the mold in the shower, they establish a trust here and buy an insurance policy there.

Typically, clients make little effort to keep those three parties informed of these changes, let alone actively bring them together as a team. For one thing, why multiply the fee? Their advisers, seeing problems and solutions from the perspective of their area of expertise, may not anticipate the impact of a solution on the future work their colleagues might engage in.

A quick math puzzle illustrates the problem. If six men digging six holes will finish in six days, how long will it take one man to dig half a hole? You might say half a day—but you would miss the fact that there is no such thing as *half a hole*. Nor is there such a thing as a partial plan.

The Solution

Working together in a collaborative environment with everyone pulling in the same direction will produce exponential results for your practice and, more importantly, for your clients.

Professional advisers know that estate planning involves both science and art so that the numbers make sense and the goals make sense—together. But for all the nuances we can design, everything derives from some combination of five core strategies to effectively reduce the value of an estate for tax purposes and to effectively fund the asset distribution and the estate tax liability that follows. The five core strategies are as follows:

- Selling assets
- Gifting assets
- Discounting assets
- Charity
- Life insurance

All informed advisers understand that these strategies can be combined to achieve results. What we cannot lose sight of—and cannot let our clients lose sight of—is that results are defined by our clients' goals, values, and circumstances and achieved by the integration of the experience and expertise of the adviser team. The strategies for the professional adviser are relatively simple. However, the lack of understanding and, therefore, implementation of the strategies takes place due to the fact the client is not as quick as the adviser at recognizing the problem. We are then left with a series of solutions to yet unrecognized problems.

Understanding our clients and integrating our efforts require a high standard of discovery.

Discovery means asking questions—building trust by patiently asking questions layer by layer and asking many of those questions again in different contexts. The same question and even the same answer will have different meanings within each adviser's area of knowledge.

Discovery also means acting as a team. Advisers have to respect each other's abilities and roles, letting go of territorial claims and egos and debates over what's right or who's right. Every adviser on the team has 100 percent input and 100 percent veto power. And every adviser has to share the same ethical standards—to work within the established framework of each profession without venturing into gray areas that put clients at risk.

The basic discovery team includes clients and spouses, CPAs, tax attorneys, and insurance advisers. It can be expanded to include business attorneys and money management advisers. In some cases, it will include clients' children. The discovery process requires a playbook shared by all parties, meetings that every team member attends, meetings to follow up on the meetings, and full communication and disclosure at every step.

What we are trying to accomplish with this deeper level of discovery is to allow the client to define their current dreams, goals, and aspirations (that is the easy part), but to also discover those that they have yet to recognize. After all, if they didn't know something was possible, how could it possibly be on their list of objectives?

Once we assist in the creation of the client's enhanced objectives, we ask that the list be prioritized by both husband and wife, then dated and signed. This way all of the advisers and the clients are working off the same menu with the same priorities and the same agenda, so we can work on the most important items first. This list or menu also serves to keep the client and the advisery team focused on what we are all trying to accomplish and reduces the risk of getting bogged down in minutia.

(continued)

(continued)

The Results

Are there really clients willing to go through this rigorous planning effort? Yes, once they see what is in it for them, or when they understand what potential traps and trouble they will avoid.

Normally, at some point in the engagement, we show a comparison to clients of what other clients have accomplished—a single slide usually tells the story. One column shows what they have achieved with their current planning. The second column shows what they can achieve with a comprehensive and integrated team of advisers. After we have been engaged and prepared a discussion draft of the new plan, we use the same type of slide to quantify the total benefits of our planning, simply and without detail so that we can see if they like the results. If they do like the results, there is plenty of time to provide them with the necessary details. If they don't like the results, you don't have to spend the time to give them details.

Current	Item	Proposed
$10,000,000	Estate Value	$10,000,000
2,000,000	Lifetime Income	2,500,000
800,000	Income Tax	500,000
3,000,000	Estate Tax	0
0	Charity	2,000,000
7,000,000	Net to Heirs	8,300,000
$ 7,000,000	Total Value	$10,300,000

We revisit that comparison repeatedly throughout the planning process to make sure the team's efforts track with those projections. We make modifications to account for new information that emerges during discovery, and we make certain clients make informed decisions about every adjusted result.

The result is a comprehensive estate plan and a commitment to monitor and modify it to adapt to changing goals, financial circumstances, economic trends, legislation, and regulation.

There are no "change orders." And nobody builds a shower that suddenly requires a whole new house.

Key Questions

Advisers should be asking their clients in similar situations the following questions:

- Although you've taken steps to protect and preserve your family's assets long term, do you have any concerns there may be gaps, and some of your goals have not yet been addressed?
- Based on your current planning, how confident are you that your assets will ultimately go to the right people at the right time in the right manner?
- You feel you have made good choices about advisers, but have you ever considered how much more value they could deliver by working as an integrated team?

Simon Singer
The Advisor Consulting Group
Encino, CA

Case Study: Business Sale Inside the Family
Making certain all family members win

Key Ideas

- Net worth primarily tied to one asset
- Equal versus fair
- Split dollar strategies

Backstory

I was introduced to the Combs family by their attorney as a result of a conversation he had at an association meeting with another attorney I have worked closely with over the years.

Sam Combs was 65 when we met, married 40 years to Bonnie. Sam owns a property development management company. It is an S corporation and accounts for nearly all of his $25+ million net worth.

The Combs have two children—Darren, age 36, who works in the family business and a daughter, Lily, 33, whose husband was transferred by his employer several states away a year before my introduction.

The Problem

Family harmony was excellent. Darren was clearly identified as the company's heir apparent, but Sam had done nothing to turn that desire into reality. Lily had no problem with her brother running the company, but she expected equal financial treatment in her parents' estate. Bonnie felt the business should go to the next generation, but she was worried about her own financial security and did not want to be a burden on her son and daughter in any way.

The company is financially sound and likely to continue to appreciate in value, so for estate planning purposes, any type of value freeze seemed desirable. However, Darren does not have significant disposable income for transfer purposes.

The Solution

The objectives we needed to accomplish included the following:

- Make certain Bonnie is independently secure for the future.
- Make certain Lily is fairly provided for.
- Ultimately transfer company ownership to Darren at the lowest possible and most reasonable cost to both parties.

- Freeze as much value as possible at Sam's death, assuming he predeceases Bonnie.
- Provide opportunities within the company for Darren to increase his net worth.
- Make certain the Combs family is not made famous in their locale because of poor planning or execution.

The company applied for $4 million of endorsement split dollar life insurance on Sam's life. Sam was insurable at standard rates, and reasonable compensation was not a problem with either Sam or Darren.

Darren entered into an agreement with the corporation providing the terms of his agreement to participate. Pursuant to the final split dollar regulations, the measure of the economic benefit are the term costs imputed to Darren. Darren received a double bonus so as not to have any after-tax outlay. The policy was issued with an increasing death benefit (Option B), and all of the equity will belong to the company. Darren will own all of the equity after rollout and will then pay the premiums of $100,000 per year. His equity is projected to increase by more than his premiums.

Meanwhile, Sam changed his estate plan to provide for Lily to receive his entire remaining unified credit in company shares at their estate tax value. She and Darren have entered into a buy-sell agreement providing Lily will sell and Darren will buy her company shares when she receives the shares, and Darren receives the life insurance proceeds. If Darren receives more in life insurance proceeds than is needed to buy Lily's shares, he must use the money to purchase shares from Sam's estate.

And beginning immediately, Darren will be a participant in some of the company's development deals in order to create greater personal net worth so he is in a stronger financial position when the business is transferred.

One more element in the case remains to be resolved. Because current split dollar regulations use Table 2001: Interim Table of One-Year Term Premiums for $1,000 of Life Insurance Protection from IRS Notice 2001–10 for calculating imputed income to the insured. At later ages, imputed income produces a very significant income tax number, which in Sam's case, breaks down the economics of the solution starting at age 92. Phase two for the Combs family plan is to establish a structure in the near future—a GRAT, qualified personal residence trust, or family limited partnership—to allow for termination of the split dollar agreement should it be necessary at that time.

(continued)

(continued)

The Result

- When Sam dies, Darren will own $4 million (or more) of shares in the family business, and Lily will have $4 million of cash.
- If Sam dies before rollout, the cash surrender value will go to the company.
- If Sam dies after the rollout, the company will have received from the life insurance company a significant share of its after-tax cost of the plan.
- If a further freeze is desired, survivor life could be purchased on the lives of Sam and Bonnie, and Darren will purchase from Sam's estate for a note shares equal to the life insurance and pay off the note when Bonnie dies.
- Bonnie can then leave cash and stock in the company to Lily with a put to Darren.
- Bonnie's estate should qualify for Internal Revenue Code Section 6166.
- The plan remains flexible to permit Sam and Bonnie to sell the business if a favorable opportunity or an unfavorable family circumstance warrants it.

Key Questions

Advisers should be asking their clients in similar situations the following questions:

- Even though the plan is to keep your business in the family, how will you balance the financial needs of the family and the business—and the IRS— when ownership transfer takes place?
- Because you have family members active in the family business as well as members who are nonactive, when it comes to distributing ownership, has it occurred to you that equal distribution may not be fair?
- Do you want to put all your company's eggs in the family succession basket, or would you rather have the flexibility to respond to other opportunities for maximizing the value of family capital?

Bart Kaufman
Kaufman Financial Corporation
Carmel, IN

Life Insurance Premium Financing and Life Settlements

8

Premium Financing

High net worth individuals who have an established need for life insurance for estate transfer or business planning purposes may be candidates for premium financing. Premium financing is a capital management tool that may allow them to leave assets intact that might be needed to pay premiums or to invest more productively assets marked for premium payments.

Sophisticated Planning for Sophisticated Clients

Clients whose estate planning requires large life insurance policies for estate liquidity can integrate premium financing into the plan if the policies are held outside the estate—most commonly in an irrevocable life insurance trust. In addition to preserving their current capital, premium financing will also provide gift tax leverage because premiums will not have to be gifted to the trust.

Businesses can also take advantage of premium financing. It can support key person coverage, buy-sell agreements, nonqualified deferred compensation, and other planning strategies.

Primary collateral for the premium finance loan is provided through cash surrender value of the financed policy. However, if the cash surrender value is less than the loan balance, additional collateral may be needed. Additional collateral may be provided in the form of a letter of credit, cash, marketable securities, or other liquid assets.

Loan interest can be repaid annually by gifts from the grantor to the trust or, if the lender agrees, can be accrued and repaid by the death benefit. Loan interest rates are commonly set using the LIBOR (London Interbank Offered Rate) plus a spread based on current market conditions.

Premium financing is a strategy limited to high net worth individuals (typically $10 million and up) who have an established need for life insurance. It is a sophisticated strategy for investors who understand the associated risks.

Managing Risks

Risks are associated with premium finance transactions. Some, but not all, of those risks include loan interest rate risk and policy crediting risk.

During the life of the loan, the loan interest rate may vary. Positive arbitrage may exist if the loan rate is less than the crediting rate on the life insurance policy. Conversely, there may be negative arbitrage if the loan rate exceeds the policy crediting rate. This risk for negative arbitrage also increases if loan interest is accrued. Proper policy design, including adding a return of premium rider or increasing the death benefit to "net" the desired amount of life insurance coverage may help mitigate these risks. Additionally, lenders may allow the loan rate to be fixed for a specified term.

Disclosure

Premium financing is complex and involves many risks, such as the possibility of policy lapse, loss of collateral, interest rate and market uncertainty, and failure to requalify with the lender to keep the financing in place and maintain the desired level of insurance protection. In certain situations, additional out-of-pocket contributions may be required to retire the debt or maintain the desired level of insurance protection, or both. A well-planned exit strategy should be in place prior to accepting any financing arrangements.

Financing is subject to the lender's collateral and financial underwriting requirements. Financing lenders typically require additional collateral during the early years of a policy in the form of cash, cash equivalents, marketable securities, a personal guaranty, or a letter of credit from a bank-approved by the lender. Interests in closely held businesses and real estate are not generally acceptable collateral. Loan interest paid by the irrevocable life insurance trust (ILIT) is not deductible.

ILIT assets may be insufficient to pay the premiums, loan interest, or repay the lender.

Pledged collateral and, in certain situations, additional out-of-pocket contributions to the ILIT, may be required to retire the debt or maintain the desired level of insurance protection, or both.

Premium financing lenders have financial underwriting and collateral requirements. Some of those considerations include:

- Cost of creating and maintaining an ILIT.
- Life insurance qualification generally requires medical and financial underwriting.
- The desired life insurance policy premium may be higher than the client's available annual gift tax exclusion or lifetime gift tax exemption, or both.
- Transfers to an ILIT are irrevocable, and the client may not possess any incidents of ownership in the life insurance policy owned by the ILIT.

Life Settlements

Before life settlements, life insurance policies were treated a lot like houses in *Monopoly*.

Suppose it's your turn, and you land on Tennessee Avenue—remember, the middle property in the orange block just before "Free Parking"? It's early in the game, and you decide to buy it.

The game progresses, and one of your playing partners buys St. James Place and New York Avenue. Meanwhile, you are running short of money, and you decide to sell Tennessee Avenue. You realize that the player who owns the other two properties in this block of three will probably pay a premium to have all three because then he can put houses down.

But when you announce you want to sell Tennessee Avenue, this player is unwilling to offer you even full board price, obviously thinking you are desperate to sell. But then another player suddenly says she will buy it at 10 percent over the board price.

What's going on? You have a market developing for Tennessee Avenue. Is this allowed by *Monopoly* rules?

When most people play *Monopoly*, they don't ever get around to selling property—the game just lasts too long to bother. But if you read the rules, unimproved property is a free market asset. You can sell Tennessee Avenue for whatever you can get.

But once you improve the property—once you put one green house on Tennessee Avenue—you can only sell that house to one entity in the game: The Bank. And the bank will pay only *one half* of the original purchase price.

Obviously, the name *Monopoly* refers to the bank.

Can you think of *any* other asset in real life that can only be sold back to the manufacturer, possibly at a fraction of the original price?

Life insurance. Until recently, that is.

Old School

For more than a century, a life insurance asset was the last thing you would sell because it was the last guarantee of financial recovery for your family if you died. In the last few decades, however, policyholders recognized that they might not need coverage, or more likely, that the policy was underperforming compared to projections at the time they bought it, and it became too expensive to maintain.

One way to resolve the problem was to quit paying premiums and let the policy lapse. If cash value was accumulated in the policy, you could surrender the policy and claim your cash surrender value. *Cash surrender value* is the amount payable to the policyholder in the event of termination or cancellation of the policy before the insured event—death.

Cash surrender value represents what you have paid into the policy—your capital—plus the credited interest minus the actuarially determined cost of coverage, and minus a surrender charge and any outstanding policy loans you may have taken.

With universal life types of policies, you have the added option of using cash value to pay for premiums until you use all the cash value up and eventually match the cost of insurance. At that point, in order to preserve the policy, you have to put in more premiums or lower the death benefit.

Either way, surrendering the policy is not very different from the *Monopoly* requirement to sell houses back to the bank at a discount.

Replacement

Of course, you could replace a poorly performing policy with a newer model that projects better performance. This would depend on whether your health had changed adversely since the current policy was purchased. But, as was explained earlier, throughout the entire life insurance industry before the 1990s, replacement was abhorred. Those agents who performed this operation repeatedly were labeled *replacement artists*— "bottom-feeding creatures" shunned by insurers and agents alike.

The indignation was justified because canceling an existing policy and purchasing another was usually in the agent's interest, *not* the client's.

But once insurers developed products in which performance risk shifted to insureds, more and more cases arose in which replacement actually *was* in the client's best interest. Insurance companies and regulators recognized they had a responsibility to support product replacement when it was in the policyholder's interest.

The problem with replacement as a tactic against poorly performing policies is that the policyholder's health may have changed enough to negatively affect new policy underwriting, limiting or even eliminating the value of the exchange. If a policyholder now has a shorter life expectancy, insurance companies cannot be expected to give them better rates than policyholders with longer life expectancy.

New Paradigm

In the 1990s, a solution did emerge and slowly became mainstream for a select segment of policyholders—a secondary market for life insurance policies known as *life settlements*. A life settlement provides policyholders a way to recover greater amounts of capital when there is no longer a need for a policy or when it is not performing as expected.

The secondary market originated in response to the AIDS/HIV outbreak, which created a need for terminally ill individuals to pay for extremely expensive care in the final stages of their lives. A market called "viatical settlements" quickly developed, which allowed insureds to sell their life insurance policies to meet this need. Third party financiers were willing to pay the insureds a significant portion of the death benefit in cash in return for the death proceeds. The short time until the anticipated mortality event created a highly predictable investment return for the financiers, but ethical considerations led to very strict guidelines for these transactions.

The innovation that came out of these transactions is now called the death benefit valuation model—a new methodology for determining the value of a life insurance policy based on the anticipated receipt of the death benefit. The acceptance of the death benefit valuation model has significantly affected the insurance landscape. Trustees and other professional advisers are now obligated to explore this new valuation approach.

In some situations, this new valuation model is more accurate than simply using the cash surrender value, as demonstrated by the example of term insurance on a terminally ill patient. Historically, term insurance has been valued at zero because it has no cash value. However, a term policy on a terminally ill patient clearly has a value even though no cash value exists. This same reasoning holds true for any insured individual who can no longer qualify medically for insurance.

The insurance marketplace refined this approach and created the life settlement market, which values any policy as the excess of the present value of the death benefit over the premiums required to sustain the policy to life expectancy. These calculations are done at the investment rate determined by the third party financier. Clearly, the most important element under this model is determining life expectancy. Independent actuarial firms have developed to meet this need, performing the same function traditionally done in the underwriting departments of life insurance companies.

A licensed broker completes the life settlement transaction, negotiating with licensed funding providers on behalf of the policyholder. Some providers use their own representatives, who work on behalf of the life settlement provider.

Providers evaluate both the policy and the policyholder's health and make offers to purchase the policy. The process requires that the provider contact the insurance company in order to evaluate the policy and obtain policyholder release of medical information to evaluate health. The provider pays the policyholder a lump sum for the determined value of the policy. Then the provider pays the premiums and eventually collects the death benefit when the insured dies.

So the risk to the provider is that the insured will outlive life expectancy and cause more premium payments before the provider receives his investment return with the death benefit. It takes good data to manage that risk, and providers focus on a general profile made up of seniors who have had negative changes in health status since their policies were issued and whose life expectancy, determined by independent review of medical records, is not longer than about 12 years. The target age is around 75 years, with a range that extends on both sides depending on circumstances.

All types of policies can qualify, including term, whole life, universal life, joint-survivorship, group, corporate-owned policies, key-man, and life policies held in irrevocable life insurance trusts. The policy owner may be the insured, a company, a family member, or a charity. Only noncontestable life insurance policies by highly rated carriers are considered, and although minimum face amounts exist, which depend on several factors, no maximums exist.

For policyholders who fit this profile, a life settlement can make sense for several circumstances and goals:

- To eliminate unaffordable premiums and recover more than would be available through policy surrender
- To purchase more cost-efficient coverage or other alternative financial products
- To purchase long-term care insurance (LTC) when it makes more financial sense than using life insurance capital to meet LTC expenses—and maintaining both is not affordable
- In the event of retiring with the right to take over key person coverage
- In the event of divorce or bankruptcy
- In the event of financial emergency

Tax Impact

Because life insurance policies are complex, the tax treatment of a life settlement can be complicated. Three general categories are defined to be considered—cash surrender value, cost basis, and settlement amount.

Two new revenue rulings add further clarification and detail to these definitions:

- Revenue Ruling 2009-13
- Revenue Ruling 2009-14

Cash surrender value is the amount of cash a policyholder receives if he or she actually terminates (surrenders) a life insurance policy before it becomes payable by death or maturity. This amount is net of any surrender charges and outstanding policy loans and interest thereon.

The taxation of the total gain (settlement proceeds less adjusted basis) is broken into two pieces: as capital gains and as ordinary income. If no cash surrender value exists or the cash surrender value is lower than the total cost basis in the policy, then the portion of the gain taxed as ordinary income is $0, and the rest would be taxed as capital gains. Otherwise, the portion of the total gain taxed as ordinary income would be the cash surrender value less the total cost basis in the policy.

If no cash surrender value exists or the cash surrender value is lower than the cost basis in the policy, then the taxable income is the dollar difference between the settlement amount and the cost basis of the policy. That amount is generally considered to be a capital gain as long as it meets the capital gain qualifications.

If the cash surrender value is higher than the cost basis, then that difference is taxed as ordinary income at the policyholder's tax bracket. Above this, the difference between the settlement amount and the cash surrender value is generally considered to be capital gain.

If the cost basis in the policy is actually higher than the settlement amount, then there should not be any taxable income from the transaction.

The number of bidders for a policy may be limited. Proceeds from sales of similar policies may vary and may be subject to claims of creditors. Receipt of proceeds may affect eligibility for government benefits and entitlements. Prior to sale, the insured should consider the continued need for coverage, affect to estate plans, availability of insurance, cost of comparable coverage, and tax implications. There may be high fees associated with the sale of a policy to the life settlement market.

Case Study: Policy Review Pays Off
Evaluating policies to maximize their value as family capital

Key Ideas

- Policy review for performance and suitability
- Insurability issues
- Life settlement

Backstory

A banker and strategic alliance partner with our firm introduced me to the Reismann family and asked me to review current life insurance policies, owned by an ILIT for their estate plan, for performance and suitability. I joined a team of advisers that already included a trustee, accountant, and attorney for the family. I added my own staff and an attorney from an insurance carrier, who is an expert in estate planning and life insurance design to the team.

Banks are very careful about objectivity in evaluating trust-owned life insurance. Generally, trust departments do not have the analytical expertise in-house, but they are wary of using agents who have the expertise if the agent may have an interest in the outcome. Our firm was chosen because we match our expertise with independence and because our interests are fully disclosed.

The Problem

The Reismann family had several life insurance issues that needed immediate attention. First, the patriarch had several life insurance policies owned by the ILIT that had not been reviewed for several years. These policies required annual premiums of $125,000 to support $6 million in death benefits.

After completing a thorough analysis of Mr. Reismann's policies, we discovered several that were either underfunded or had adequate dividends to subsidize the ongoing premiums. Mr. Reismann's health had declined in recent years, which made him an uninsurable risk from the insurer's point of view but could increase the value of his policies for a life settlement transaction.

The Decision Process

We solicited the secondary marketplace to test whether we could sell the policies and use the proceeds in more advantageous ways for the estate. Offers from the

(continued)

(continued)

secondary market depend on independent life expectancy estimates and, in this case, the two life expectancy companies both quoted eight years. So we compared the offers for the sale of the policies against keeping the policies—in other words, the projected growth of the proceeds of the sale at a reasonable rate of return over eight years versus the cost of maintaining the policies through dividends and premiums for the death benefit in eight years. The internal rate of return analysis heavily favored keeping the policies, which was the recommendation the team agreed on. In addition, we were able to "tweak" his existing contracts to reduce his annual premiums down to $40,000 from $125,000.

This was a good test of objectivity for two reasons. Keeping the policies in place established our firm's financial neutrality in the decision since compensation continued for the agents of record. But also, I had recused my firm from any income that would have resulted from the sale of the policies in the secondary market. The Reismann family was well-served, and the bank fulfilled its fiduciary obligations.

Equally important, the Reismanns and the members of the team respected how I facilitated the very delicate subjects that had to be addressed openly, like discussing your life expectancy in terms of an eight-year "quote." I was able to ask the tough questions and effectively moved the decision process from emotional to financial, quarterbacking the team through issues that had always been avoided.

The family also had a $10 million generation-skipping trust that was set up by Mr. Reismann's father that was mainly invested in stocks and bonds. After reviewing the trust documents, I found that the trust permitted the purchase of life insurance on Mr. and Mrs. Reismann. We illustrated for the family and the team the benefits of buying life insurance within a funded trust. The team agreed that the strategy was a home run for the Reismann family—a bases-loaded home run because Mrs. Reismann was underwritten as a preferred risk for the survivorship policy. They agreed to reallocate $150,000 of annual income from the trust to buy a $9 million policy.

The Result

The Reismanns gained significant financial benefits for the family. We reduced their annual premiums, which in turn, reduced their gift tax exposure. We created two separate "second-to-die" policies that will serve as an alternative investment, as well as a wealth replacement vehicle. Finally, we instituted an Insurance Policy

Statement to match their Investment Policy Statement, mandating annual review of policies and policy management.

Key Questions

Advisers should be asking their clients in similar situations the following questions:

- When was the last time you revisited your estate plan in the context of policy evaluation?
- Have you investigated all opportunities to maximize the value of current policies, whether they are underperforming or not, suitable or not?
- Are you aware that medical advances have created a new underwriting environment, replacing assumptions about insurability with new sets of facts?

Jay Cavanagh, CRFA
The KNW Group, LLC
Minnetonka, MN

Case Study: Two Stones, Many Birds
Achieving diverse wealth transfer goals in one comprehensive plan

Key Ideas

- Integrated wealth transfer planning
- Grantor retained annuity trusts (GRATs)
- Gifting strategies

Background

The client is an auto dealer with multiple dealerships worth over $100 million in 2003. Pete Parnell and his wife Carla have three sons—one of whom is currently active and the planned future successor.

The Parnells wanted to transfer the dealerships to the children on the most tax advantageous basis both during lifetime and at death. Therefore, planning for the estate costs was paramount. In addition, they wanted to protect the active child while being fair to the children who were not active in the dealerships.

Pete also owns the dealership properties. Through earlier planning, we helped him transfer these properties to two limited liability companies (LLCs). After outright gifts to the three children, Pete retained a 4 percent managing member interest in one LLC and a 40 percent interest in the other. The value for both interests on a discounted basis amounted to $25 million. The only other assets in the estate are the home and notes receivable from the dealerships totaling over $10 million. Thus, not only was the estate illiquid, but all the assets were tied-up in the business and subject to the ongoing success of the dealerships.

The Parnells had over $15 million of life insurance purchased in our prior planning—$10 million of survivor life and $5 million on Pete's life alone. These policies were held in an insurance trust created in the early 1980s and funded on a split dollar basis, then subsequently converted to the loan regime in 2003. The insurance trust was neither a grantor trust nor did it have generation skipping provisions. The immediate liquidity needs would be over $50 million to pay the estate taxes at the second death.

Problems

The estate taxes would most likely cause some or all of the dealerships to be sold maybe at distressed prices and certainly not within the timeframe of the appropriate valuation dates (date of death or six months later). Therefore, the planning would involve two main objectives, prioritized by the client:

- Find a way to minimize the estate tax liability.
- Provide sufficient liquidity to pay the resulting estate taxes after implementation of any tax reduction techniques.

Secondary objectives included an exit strategy for the policies funded under the loan regime. And finally, due to the makeup of the assets (all business related), we needed to address the ultimate distribution to insure that the active child had control of the dealerships while treating the two nonactive children fairly.

Solutions

1. Estate reduction to minimize transfer taxes

After looking at many estate freezing and reducing techniques, the Parnells decided to utilize two GRATs to transfer the majority of Pete's stock ownership to his three sons, one on his life and one on his wife's life both for six-year terms. These were structured as Walton type GRATs in which the gift was minimized based on the cash flows relative to the value of the stock being gifted.

Two steps were critical before implementing the GRATs. First, the stock of the dealerships was converted to 2 percent voting and 98 percent nonvoting shares—all of the dealerships were S corporations. Next, an appraisal of all the dealerships was conducted, valuing the 98 percent interests with appropriate discounts—lack of control and marketability. The appraisals were fairly aggressive, bringing the value of the nonvoting interests in all dealerships down to about $50 million. At these values, and with the assumed cash flow from the S corporations able to support a rather large annuity payment, each GRAT resulted in just a $20,000 gift allocable against the Parnell's lifetime exemptions.

The Parnells had utilized $600,000 each of their lifetime exemptions from our prior planning as gifts of LLC interests to the children in 1999. Because only $20,000 each was being used for the implementation of the GRATs, it made sense to look at utilizing the remaining exemptions of $380,000 each to help with additional planning, including the exit strategy for the loan regime policies.

2. Insurance trust structured as grantor trust

We illustrated the numerous benefits of a grantor trust, not just as an estate tax reduction vehicle but also as a funding source for life insurance and, therefore,

(continued)

(continued)

as a source for an exit strategy as well. We also illustrated the advantage of having life insurance in a trust that is generation skipping tax exempt. As a result, the Parnell's attorney created a new insurance trust that was a grantor trust and incorporated generation skipping provisions.

To fund the new trust initially, the client gifted a 5 percent interest in one of his dealerships and a 1 percent interest in one of the real estate LLCs—a gift tax value of $700,000 or $350,000 each. This allowed for the new trust to purchase the policies from the old trust, subject to an assumption of the existing loans under the loan regime. The purchase price was based on the account values of the policies less the loans assumed by the new trust. The policies were purchased under a nine-year note with interest at the applicable federal rate. The transfer-for-value rule did not apply for two reasons: the trust was a grantor trust, and as a backup, the gift of the 1 percent interest in the LLC qualified the trust as a "partner" and an exempt transferee.

Now we had a trust that held income-producing assets generating just over $200,000 per year in income. Because it was a grantor trust, Pete (grantor) was responsible for paying the income taxes on all the trust income, the equivalent of an annual $80,000 tax-free gift ($200,000 @ 40% tax rate). In addition, the Parnells were able to gift $240,000 per year to the trust using their annual exclusions with10 real beneficiaries because it was a generation skipping trust. The total of over $440,000 per year to the trust—income and gifts—allowed for the start of the exit strategy for the loan regime.

The annual premiums for the existing $15 million of life insurance were about $200,000. The note payments for the purchase of the policies from the old trust amounted to $30,000 per year. This left about $210,000 per year to pay the interest and a portion of the principal on the loans outstanding under the split dollar loan regime. Assuming a steady cash flow in the future, the loans for both the purchase of the policies and the loan regime would be fully repaid by 2012.

3. Liquidity needs addressed

One of the remaining problems was the liquidity shortfall if Pete and Carla did not survive the GRAT terms of six years. A portion of the GRATs assets are includable in their estate. This contingency was addressed through the purchase of additional life insurance. In this case, the wife's health had worsened since the original purchase of insurance in 2002. In addition, the need for insurance may only be temporary because the GRATs would remove most of the Parnells' net worth from their estates if they survived the term. Pete was 82, so term insurance was not an option. Based on the previous information, we felt it was best to purchase universal life insurance on Pete's life only, with the ability to tap the secondary market if he felt he no longer needed the insurance after the GRAT term. This potential secondary market option made the insurance purchase decision easier for the Parnells. Our feeling is that even after the GRATs mature, the need for some, if not all, the insurance will still exist.

Therefore, Pete decided to purchase an additional $25 million to cover the mortality risk of the GRATs. He decided to prefund three years' worth of premiums initially to coincide with the dates the GRATs matured (the insurance was purchased in 2006). This approach allows them to decide after three years whether to continue funding the premiums, surrender the contracts, or sell them under a life settlement. The premiums for this coverage were $900,000 and would have required either taxable gifts, more loans from the corporation funding the original split dollar plan, or some form of financing. We recommended private financing.

Private financing was attractive to the Parnells for many reasons. First, he could loan personally to the trust at the then very low applicable federal rates and lock the interest rate in for a nine-year period (mid-term rate). Next, the interest could accrue without any adverse income or gift taxation to the Parnells or the trust. This was key because it would not require any current cash flow and allowed for a quicker pay down of the traditional split dollar loans, which were not as tax efficient as the private financed loans. Finally, the exit strategy for these loans would be accomplished, worst case scenario, when the GRATs matured.

Because one cannot allocate the goods and services tax (GST) exemption to a GRAT gift until the GRAT matures, beneficiaries of GRATS typically are not GST exempt trusts. In this case, the GRAT beneficiary was a non-GST trust that mirrored the new life insurance trust. Once the GRATs mature, GRAT assets flow to these non-GST trusts. These trusts could then loan money to the insurance trust to be able to pay the Parnells back, if needed. Otherwise, the loans could continue to accrue until the earlier of the end of the term (ninth year) or the client's death.

4. Significant tax-free gifts created

The gifts of stock to the insurance trust along with the GRATs were complete in the summer of 2003. Gift tax returns were filed in April of 2004 with complete disclosure—a stack of documents about three feet high. Because Pete was

(continued)

(continued)

never audited and the statute of limitations expired in April 2007, the transactions cannot be challenged. Recently, he sold one of his dealerships for $45 million. It so happens this is also the dealership in which the insurance trust owns a 5 percent interest. Therefore, the trust will receive $2.25 million in sales proceeds. In addition, Pete will pay the capital gains tax on behalf of the trust equal to approximately $500,000, the equivalent of a $500,000 tax-free gift to the trust because of the grantor status of the trust.

Because the insurance trust keeps the entire sales proceeds of $2.25 million, it will use these proceeds to completely repay the split dollar loans. This will free up the $210,000 of cash flow currently being used to pay down the split dollar loans for other uses. This can help pay future premiums if Pete decides to continue the insurance. His current objective is to keep the insurance because he believes it is a good investment. Otherwise, it can be used to repay a portion of the loans due the Parnells from the private financing or as funding for another investment such as real estate. Furthermore, the GRATs will receive proceeds amounting to $41,850,000 from the sale of one of the dealerships, and the Parnells will pay in excess of $6.5 million in capital gains tax, which will amount to another tax-free gift to the trust due to its grantor status.

Summary

We were able to work with the client to accomplish many of the following objectives with two main tools—life insurance and grantor trusts:

- Sufficient liquidity was provided in the event of the client's death, whenever that were to occur.
- Tremendous value will be transferred in 2009 after the GRATs mature with virtually no gift involved ($40,000 of total gifts between husband and wife to move over $100 million worth of dealership stock and cash from the sale of one of the dealerships). This will save tens of millions in future estate taxes.
- Split dollar loans have been paid in full (completing the split dollar exit strategy implemented back in 2003 after converting to the loan regime).
- The insurance that would have been taxable in the children's estates are now sheltered in a new GST exempt insurance trust.
- The grantor trust status of the new insurance trust affords many of the following advantages:
  — By paying the income taxes on trust income, the client is making tax-free "gifts" that assist in making premium payments on the life insurance.

— Private financing gifts from the grantor can accrue interest without any adverse income or gift taxation to the grantor or the trust.

— Sales of assets by the trust are tax-free to the trust (taxes paid by grantor).

— The trust has a self-funding mechanism for insurance premiums.

Key Questions

Advisers should be asking their clients in similar situations the following questions:

- Have you reviewed your estate plan to make sure that tax, financial, or personal changes haven't turned yesterday's solutions into tomorrow's problems?
- If comprehensive estate planning seems too involved right now, shouldn't you at least look into a what-if estate plan that tells you where your risks lie?
- Because you want all of your children to be future owners of your business, but not all of them will be active in management, have you planned for what potential conflicts among active and inactive owners might do to the business and the family?

Kyle DeVries and Bob Kelly
Creative Edge Planning
Westlake Village, CA

Case Study: Policies in Remission
Preserving life insurance capital in ailing policies

Key Ideas

- Repair strategies for loan-impaired policies
- Alternatives for underfunded but necessary policies
- Life settlement

Backstory #1

We had an ongoing client relationship with the Ogden family, although Mr. Ogden also uses several other firms like ours in our region. We knew his attorney, accountant, and trustee directly through mutual clients.

The Problem

Mr. and Mrs. Ogden had two identical joint life trust-owned life insurance policies, purchased in 1989 through another firm. They were heavily financed using heavy internal policy loans, and while as originally illustrated, these policies would hold up under current assumptions, new in force illustrations projected additional premium recurring. Because Mrs. Ogden is 20 years younger than her husband, they are concerned about the amount of future premium needed after he was gone. He wanted to leave a policy and plan in place that would not require additional premiums or activity.

When we reviewed the insurance portfolio we found policies with existing policy loans in addition to these two. Mr. Ogden did not fully understand the consequences of loans and the possible long-term effect.

We ran in force ledgers of all policies showing no additional outlays. Under current assumptions, the policies would remain in force, with lower net death benefit amounts. However, the accruing policy loans were troubling because at Mrs. Ogden's life expectancy, these loans would accumulate to over $50 million. If the products do not perform as currently illustrated, and the Ogdens did not pay additional premiums, the policy could lapse without value *and* produce a 1099 of taxable phantom income of tens of millions of dollars.

The Solution

We recommended restructuring the policies to remove the policy loans and transfer to a lower death benefit guaranteed product with no additional premiums.

Before we performed the 1035 exchange of the existing policies, we used internal paid-up additions to reduce the policy loan without affecting the net cash surrender value. The result was loan amounts that were more manageable for the exchange. Then we waited an appropriate amount of time before we executed the 1035 exchange and designed a new plan that solved for a maximum guaranteed death benefit in the new policy using the net surrender value transferred, assuming no additional premiums and the loan to be paid off at the beginning of the second policy anniversary.

At the beginning of the second policy anniversary, we directed the remaining loan to be paid off using internal policy values. The Ogdens now had an ongoing policy that eliminated the loans and was guaranteed to remain in force with no additional premiums. Though the total death benefit was initially lower, over the long term, the Ogdens felt the greater value was the security that the policy will remain in force with no additional premiums and no worry of phantom income.

One last note: the agent that had formerly placed the loan impaired coverage took the reasonable step on behalf of the Ogdens of hiring a third party consultant to review our process and challenge the replacements. The consultant agreed with our implementation decision and signed off for Mr. and Mrs. Ogden to approve the transaction.

Backstory #2

Ms. Ingram was 89 years old and the remaining survivor of a trust-owned joint life policy benefiting the grandchildren of the deceased joint-insured. However, she had not been married to the insured and was not related to the trust beneficiaries. Her trustee and attorney introduced us to her.

The Problem

Ms. Ingram and her advisers were concerned that the second-to-die life insurance policy was thinly funded and required significant ongoing premium support. The joint insured had funded the premiums paid by the trust during his lifetime, but he died without a plan for paying premiums after his death.

The policy had a $13.9 million face amount, cash value of less than $800,000, and an ongoing annual premium requirement of about $1.3 million. Because neither the trustee, the beneficiaries, nor Ms. Ingram had the means to pay the ongoing premiums, there was a real risk that the policy would lapse without value. Everyone recognized that the joint insured would not have wanted his financial legacy for his grandchildren lost.

(continued)

(continued)

The Solution

We examined three potential solutions simultaneously:

- Reducing the death benefit, assuming no additional premiums
- Premium financing
- Life settlement

Due to the small current cash surrender value, reducing the face amount produced only a small multiple of the current cash surrender value and turned out to not be a viable alternative.

Premium financing was not an option because none of the potential sponsors of the plan could offer the collateral necessary to support the minimal projected ongoing cash value even with future premiums.

On the life settlement side, we worked with several brokers to obtain life expectancy estimates. An average life expectancy for Ms. Ingram was 5.5 years. Then we initiated a competitive bidding process. After about 6 weeks, we were able to solicit offers to the client. They began low as $1.2 million, but a top bid of $4.63 million was acceptable to all parties. They now have a substantial benefit and are relieved of the obligation to fund ongoing premiums they could not afford. The majority of the life settlement compensation was a tax-free return of basis; the remaining compensation was taxed at the capital gains rate.

Key Questions

Advisers should be asking their clients in similar situations the following questions

- Have you reviewed your life insurance policies to make sure your funding strategies are still viable?
- What contingency plan do you have to meet future premium obligations if your policies do not perform as projected?
- If you have a joint life policy that requires additional premiums in the future, do you have a funding plan for each of the joint lives?
- Are you aware that you can now preserve the value of life insurance capital by selling a policy in the secondary market if circumstances make that the most favorable option?

Don Payne
Harris, Crouch, Long, Scott & Miller, Inc.
Whitsett, NC

Private Placement Life Insurance and Corporate and Bank Owned Life Insurance (COLI/BOLI)

9

Private placement variable life insurance offers advantages for wealthy investors, and professional advisers need to understand the advantages to decide which clients could benefit.

To understand the concept of private placement applied to life insurance, follow the development of life insurance products in terms of policyholder risk. With pure term insurance, the risk to meet death benefit obligations rests entirely on the insurance company. Whole life policies added the risk of accumulation guarantees. Then insurers unbundled the death benefit and cash accumulation components with universal life, allowing policyholders to manage within limits the amount of premium and putting the risk of maintaining the death benefit in the policyholders' hands. Variable universal life (VUL) took that flexibility one step further by unbundling investment choice from the company's general account into separate accounts managed by policyholders, adding investment risk to the policyholder side of the contract.

Two decades of economic growth helped establish VUL as a very attractive product for sophisticated insurance buyers. The downturn that followed made managing investments more challenging, but VUL remained an effective solution for many long-term insurance planning needs.

However, to sophisticated investors, VUL is like an off-the-rack suit when they are used to ordering custom tailored suits. VUL is a regulated product that must be registered with the Securities and Exchange Commission and state insurance commissioners, but the private placement VUL is fully negotiable for high net worth consumers. Examples of VUL include:

- Sales loads
- Fees instead of commissions
- Maintenance and expense risk charges
- Surrender charges
- Investment choices, subject to tax rules

Managing this list of variables goes over the heads of nearly all clients and most of their advisers—in fact, it goes over the heads of the majority of life insurance agents,—and mistakes will be costly. Customizing a life insurance policy by manipulating these variables can result in a contract that no longer qualifies as a life insurance contract, sacrificing significant tax advantages.

Complicating the picture further is the second level of decision-making after product design. Private placement variable life insurance can be purchased from offshore insurers in addition to domestic ones. Although offshore insurers are not allowed to solicit business in the United States, residents can purchase life insurance from them through informed agents.

In such a case, tax advantages will remain the same whether the product comes from a foreign or domestic insurer. However, foreign companies may offer lower costs by not having to pay U.S. premium tax and other factors, allowing more premiums to go into the investment component of the policy and potentially earn higher returns. Of course, foreign insurers may have other taxes to pay or may incur higher costs in other areas.

Another advantage can be access to more sophisticated investments. Although domestic insurers continue to widen the spectrum of invest-ment choices, offshore companies have had an edge in the past.

In spite of these potential advantages, a foreign life insurance policy comes with risks similar to any foreign investment. Less regulation might seem like an advantage if it produces lower cost or higher returns, but regulation is equally a good thing in terms of consumer protections. For one thing, it provides the basis for consistent ratings of companies. In addition to management issues, foreign companies may be subject to much higher risks of political and economic change, making thorough evaluation of claims-paying ability and financial strength paramount.

Who gets to take advantage of the custom tailoring of life insurance policies and foreign versus domestic carriers? Only someone meeting the *Qualified Purchaser* criteria under the Investment Company Act of 1940 and the *Accredited Investor* criteria under the Securities Act of 1933 and, practically speaking, only someone investing a large amount in the policy and possessing the business or financial experience to understand what they are buying.

The next question is who should manage the purchase for them. Given the intricate design and purchase decisions, a substantial education process becomes critical. This transfer of knowledge requires an adviser who can function at an expert level and can communicate knowledge effectively to nonexperts—both clients and the members of their advisery teams.

Private Placement Disclosure

Private placement is the term used in the securities world to define a nonpublic offering of an investment vehicle. Securities regulations allow exemption for selected types of private placements. The primary classifications for these exemptions are Rules 501-506, Regulation D of the Securities Act of 1933. Smaller private offerings can be done when there are less than 35 investors and when the public is not solicited (for example, friends and family rounds of financing). The most common types of private placements are those involving closely-held private companies. Private placements are not suitable for many investors. The Private Placement Memorandum is a disclosure document that includes the details and potential risk scenarios of the offering and the financial condition of the company. The Private Placement Memorandum is required so that potential investors understand the nature of and the risks associated with the investment. The Private Placement Memorandum contains information required by law that must be provided to unaccredited investors and should be provided to accredited investors so they can make an informed decision whether or not to participate.

Corporate/Bank Owned Life Insurance (COLI/BOLI)

Both Corporate and Bank Owned Life Insurance are products that were specifically created for the institutional use of life insurance by organizations to finance, offset, or cost-recover certain tangible and intangible liabilities.

COLI

COLI has a long history as funding for the costs associated with the loss of key employees due to death or disability and the need to repurchase stock from shareholders to fulfill buy-sell agreements.

In addition, corporations purchase life insurance as a funding mechanism related to the cost of employee benefits, qualified plans, health plans, postretirement benefit obligations, and other benefit liabilities.

COLI has long played an important informal financing role in nonqualified plans, matching assets to liabilities in executive benefits, deferred compensation, supplemental executive retirement plans, and carve-out plans. Many of these companies choose COLI as the financing vehicle because the growth in the COLI is tax-deferred and the cash proceeds, when received by the company as borrowings from the policies, are income tax free. Additionally, death benefits upon the death of the insured are income tax free subject to compliance with Internal Revenue Code (IRC) Section 101(j). IRC Sections 101(j) and 6039I, enacted on August 17, 2006, as part of the Pension Protection Act of 2006, included new rules with respect to the taxation of death benefit proceeds of an "employer-owned" life insurance policy. IRC Section 101(j) now subjects death benefits on employer-owned life insurance policies to income taxation to the extent they exceed the employer's basis in the policy, unless (1) a valid exception applies, and (2) notice and consent requirements are satisfied.

In addition, companies can recognize in their financial statements the increase in cash surrender value each year, as follows:

- COLI can earn a higher after-tax yield than taxable investments.
- COLI matches the long-term nature of benefit plan expenses.
- COLI assets can be matched with benefit liabilities for better asset liability management.

Often this is a source of confusion for plan sponsors, arising from other qualified plans that sit off the employer balance sheet and, in many instances, require no asset liability management, such as a 401(k) plan. However, nonqualified plan liabilities and informal funding assets sit on the corporation's balance sheet. The fact that the plan liabilities and informal funding assets are on the balance sheet simply means that the company "feels" any economic mismatch on either a positive or negative basis.

BOLI

For over three decades, banks have utilized BOLI portfolios because regulators have provided clear guidance on the use of this asset class by banking organizations, per OCC Bulletin 2004-56. During the past decade, usage rates among banks have soared so that today BOLI is a feature of the balance sheets of a majority of banking organizations.

Primarily, BOLI is used to offset new or existing nonqualified benefit plan expenses or to offset the costs of existing benefit plan expenses and is most commonly designed as a single premium life insurance modified endowment contract. The primary benefits of BOLI include the following:

- Tax-advantaged increases in cash value
- Tax-free death benefit proceeds
- Issued by highly rated insurance companies
- Ability to select underlying asset characteristics

Mechanics of COLI and BOLI

Both BOLI and COLI function in a similar manner. The process is as follows:

- Corporation or bank is the owner, premium payer, and beneficiary of the policy.
- Group of highly compensated executives are insured (in concert with COLI Best Practices language).
- Asset accumulates based on selected product or underlying fund.
- Asset may be withdrawn or loaned out from the policy to pay certain benefits on a tax free basis (COLI only).
- Mortality events create cash flows of the policy on a tax free basis.

Institutionally Priced Products

Life insurance owned by corporations and banks is a specialized niche market primarily served by the largest carriers, and their products tend to share the following features in common.

Pricing

Pricing for institutional products is based on a more selective risk class with higher life expectancy than the retail risk pool class, allowing lower cost of insurance. Other pricing factors related to marketing and administration costs also tend to be lower. As a result, unlike retail policies, these institutional polices offer close to or in excess of 100 percent cash surrender value to premium ratio in the first year.

Underwriting Programs

As the number of lives insured increases, so does the potential for guaranteed issue, usually at 10–15 lives or more. Guaranteed issue involves no medical exams or medical questions for participants in a COLI/BOLI program.

Product Choice

Typically COLI/BOLI is available in fixed account, registered product, or private placement designs.

Planning Considerations

With nonqualified plans, plan sponsors have three of the following primary choices about funding issues.

Unfunded

The opportunity to achieve some short-term cash flow benefits may make not funding a benefits program seem attractive. However, in the mid to long run, the economic impacts can make that decision less attractive, if future management is subjected to much more significant cash flow problems when benefit payments are required. In the contractual agreements in deferred compensation plans, participants are in an unsecured creditor position if bankruptcy were to occur, so lack of funding can detract from the perceived value of the plan from a participant's standpoint.

Funded With Taxable Assets

This alternative provides benefit security. However, two key drawbacks are taxes and generally accepted accounting principles (GAAP) accounting. These informal assets sit on the balance sheet, so the spin-off of taxable income and accounting in accordance with Financial Accounting Standards Board (FASB) Statement No. 115, *Accounting for Certain Investments in Debt and Equity Securities* (codified in FASB *Accounting Standards Codification* (ASC) 320, *Investments—Debt and Equity Securities*), make this asset a less attractive alternative from an economic perspective.

Tax-Advantaged COLI Assets

The third alternative adds a thin layer of complexity of funding due to the nature of the insurance component, but it has one of the best economic and overall asset liability management profiles of any of the alternatives.

With informal funding assets being a part of the company's general balance sheet, taxes produced from the funding asset are a key consideration. The impacts of informally funding a plan with a tax advantaged COLI asset versus taxable assets can be significant.

GAAP accounting and accounting in accordance with FASB Statement No. 115 can also play a major role. The available-for-sale treatment of securities essentially means that only realized gains pass through the income statement, whereas unrealized gains flow through to shareholder's equity. This accounting difference can create "gaps" in income and expenses for the informal funding asset and the plan liabilities on the income statement, whereas life insurance is subject to FASB Technical Bulletin 85-4, *Accounting for Purchases of Life Insurance* (codified in FASB ASC 325-30), which provides for mark to market accounting treatment.

Case Study: Don't Forget the Nonprofit Sector
Helping both donors and nonprofit leaders

Key Ideas

- Leveraging an IRA into a major charitable gift.
- IRC Section 457(f) risk of forfeiture issues in top hat plans.
- IRC Section 409A regulations hit nonprofits too.
- Reasonable compensation morphs into private inurement.

Backstory #1

Louis Varney has been a client of our firm for 15 years, and since he sold his business for a considerable sum, a major focus of his life has been charitable goals. His estate planning is well-developed and continually monitored, but I knew he was always looking for ways to give more away.

Lou has a $3.5 million IRA. He did things right—systematically building a qualified savings asset, but at the same time, building enough personal net worth not to need it. For now, he wants to keep the balance so that his wife can look forward to a liquid asset if she needs it, but he realizes that the IRA will be taxed under both estate tax and income tax rules at the second death. So it makes more tax sense and serves his charitable goals to designate a charity as the beneficiary.

The Problem

The limitations on annual charitable giving don't allow Lou to make a large disbursement from the IRA without having all of the funds treated as income, and it is quite likely that a portion of the funds won't be deductible under the 50 percent rule. Moreover, once he turns 70½, there will be minimum required distributions that effectively impair the IRA's ability to grow to a very large amount for charity at death. So I asked him if he would like to hear ways to preserve liquidity and also maximize his charitable potential using the IRA.

The Decision Process

His answer was yes, and the recommendation was very simple. We compared his present IRA planning versus two alternative approaches designed to deliver the maximum amount to charity while still leaving a balance in the IRA in case it was needed by a surviving spouse. The difference was stunning.

The first idea was the systematic distribution of annual amounts from the IRA to the investment fund in Lou's private foundation. But this solution created another problem. The 5 percent distribution rule for foundations did not allow the foundation to grow as much as Lou wanted.

Instead, we applied the foundation's annual deposits from the IRA to a life insurance policy owned by the foundation. This policy was carefully designed to have an increasing death benefit, variable premium schedule, and a positive but low cash value. The increasing death benefit and variable premium allowed the flexibility to deliver required minimum distributions at whatever amount was required. The low cash value reduced the amount that would otherwise drive up the 5 percent required distributions from the foundation.

The Result

Even if Lou and his wife both survive to age 99, their gift to charity will improve from a projected $12 million to charity to almost $33 million to charity. In all prior years, the charitable result is better by at least $11 million.

They are assured a significant charitable legacy, but the systematic approach allows him to change his mind in any year and reduce the program to a lower level if liquidity issues come up. The charitable amounts do not cause any feeling of "disinheritance" for their children, and the assets used to accomplish the client's charitable giving are the qualified plan assets that are often devalued for the next generation by taxation.

Backstory #2

The implementation of this idea next led to an introduction to one of the charities that would be the beneficiary of the Varneys' charitable legacy. Lou is a board member of a ministry forcefully led by Larry Townsend.

Larry had done no personal retirement planning, but his board had initiated and promoted to the donors a retirement fund for Larry to be held in a rabbi trust. The fund receives gifts from donors interested in this specific need, and between $1 million and $2 million has been pledged over the next five years.

However, no one had any idea that when the retirement benefit would begin to be paid out, the IRS would assess ordinary income taxes on the *present value of the anticipated income*, not just on the first year benefit.

(continued)

(continued)

The Problems

This is the special trap built into IRC Section 457(f) once an employee of a nonprofit no longer has a risk of forfeiture. For example, a nonprofit leader might qualify for a 20-year retirement benefit of $100,000 per year, but his taxable income upon retiring and having no more risk of forfeiture could easily be around $1 million. Where does he find the $350,000+ to pay this tax?

On top of the Section 457(f) problem, nonprofit leaders typically have retirement plans that are likely to be outside of the new IRC Section 409A requirements. They had until the end of 2008 to bring their plans into compliance. This meant they would have far less flexibility in timing or structuring how they would receive their retirement account. This means they will have far less flexibility in timing or structuring how they will receive their retirement account.

As we looked more deeply, a third critical issue appeared—reasonable compensation. With the nonprofit leader already age 62, could we fund a meaningful retirement benefit without escalating the required funding beyond what would be considered reasonable compensation? Similarly, would such a plan be considered private inurement? Crossing this line could jeopardize the organization's tax status and trigger ugly taxes on the organization and even on the directors personally.

The Planning Process

The entire board of directors reviewed a number of summaries and analyses of the interplay of Sections 457(f) and 409A. They considered Mr. Townsend's total compensation package and compared it with compensation earned by other leaders of similar organizations. The ministry has a strong and very competent board with a top attorney who took the lead with us on the technical issues so that the other board members could make informed decisions. The board agreed to pursue the planning process and stipulated retaining an outside compensation expert to assure that the plan would not cross the unreasonable compensation line.

We developed several options for the board to consider, including the following:

- Preapproval of a loan to cover the taxes at retirement
- Preapproval of a bonus to cover the taxes at retirement including taxes on the bonus
- Use of a restricted bonus plan that passes the unreasonable compensation test
- Split dollar life insurance updated to current rules

After detailed consideration of the options, the solution that made the most sense followed bullet two, shown previously. Mr. Townsend recused himself, and all of the independent directors approved the plan.

The Solution

The plan provides Larry Townsend a promised retirement benefit equal to a percentage of compensation, payable for life, beginning at age 70, with a provision to allow a lump sum benefit at age 70. In addition the plan funds a tax bonus to cover the 457(f) problem.

To satisfy the new requirements of 409A, a new employment agreement was required. Due to the short funding period, large annual funding contributions are required. The benefit funding utilizes the existing rabbi trust, amended to fit with the employment agreement.

Here's how the retirement plan works:

- The ministry receives contributions for the retirement fund.
- A separate "bonus fund" collects all transfers of contributions from the ministry to the rabbi trust.
- The bonus fund makes deposits into the benefits fund on an annual basis and invests the balance of the funds with an investment objective consistent with a projected payout in year 2015.
- A secondary objective is to deliver a spousal benefit if Townsend were to die prematurely.
- Annual deposits to the benefits fund are made into a COLI policy, the same policy used in for-profit companies.

    COLI funding offers several benefits based on life insurance tax structure and policy design.
- Cash values are invested in variable portfolios and grow tax deferred inside the policy (not an issue for funds inside a nonprofit, but a very big issue when, in the future, the policy is owned by the executive).
- Policy could be given to exec at any age (70 in this case), for the delivery of tax free retirement income.
- Projected income is slightly higher than could be earned with common investments by taking advantage of COLI tax-deferral and lower fund fees.
- Larry Townsend will also benefit from the creditor protection status of life insurance available under the laws of his particular state.

(continued)

(continued)

Lessons Learned

Sometimes the numbers don't matter when your retirement plan is poorly designed and exposed to unexpected taxes plus compliance issues. In this case, the client was able to have a well-designed retirement plan with a good benefit *and* the upfront taxes prefunded in a separate account. By doing things right, the nonprofit entity is in a position to attract the best leadership and assure the donors that their contributions are being used wisely.

By using an insurance product, we are able to deliver both a higher annual income plus a death benefit if the insured doesn't survive to his retirement date. The insurance actually beat a 9 percent hypothetical investment fund. We have also created a situation in which, at retirement, Larry Townsend will be able to have his entire retirement account transferred from the ministry to a creditor-proof, personally owned structure. From there, he can tailor his annual income payments to fit his needs without any of the "fixed" demands of Section 409A (amounts and timing of distributions). He also escapes the economic risks that the organization might face after his retirement has begun.

The development of a retirement plan for a nonprofit leader can be tricky, but if it is done correctly, everyone wins. The organization will have a happy leader who is much more likely to continue to serve all the way up to his retirement. The board will know that it has done its job for the leader personally and for the organization. The worry of a heavy tax burden appearing the moment the leader begins to collect his retirement benefit is removed.

Key Questions

Advisers should be asking their clients in similar situations the following questions:

- Would you be interested in increasing your ability to give to charity without affecting your financial security during your lifetime or the financial security of your children long term?
- Would you like to guarantee the highest possible delivery of funds to a charity no matter when you die?
- Do the committed leaders of the charitable organizations your legacy serves have personal financial plans that are fully integrated with the organization they serve?
- Does your organization understand all the special opportunities as well as compensation tax traps unique to nonprofits?

- Are the organizations you support doing everything they can to attract and retain the best leadership?
- Are they taking care of their leadership financially so that the leaders can fully focus their attention on the mission of the organization?

Gregory C. Freeman
Strategic Stewardship
Woodstock, GA

Case Study: S Corporation Sale Funded by Tax Savings
Setting the clock for business transition

Key Ideas

- Business continuity alternatives.
- S Corporation employee stock ownership plan (ESOP).
- Business planning determines estate planning.

Backstory

We met Stuart Mortensen through his banker, who had attended one of our seminars on ESOPs. The bank had served the family business for two generations, and even though Stuart was now in his 60s, no plan was in place for the third generation, nor were there any other transition options under consideration. The banker was concerned that without a plan, the business would end up being sold to a competitor or simply liquidated.

We learned from Stuart that he did not want to sell to an outsider. But by now, all the family member candidates were committed to their own careers, so Stuart wanted the business to go to the people who had committed themselves to it for years—the key employees. It was a noble sentiment, but none of the management team had financial resources to accomplish that goal, and Stuart definitely wanted to get his capital out at the sale.

The Problem

When we gathered more facts about Stuart's personal financial history, we were struck by how little estate planning he had engaged in, let alone completed. For example, in a few years, he would begin required minimum distributions from an IRA of very substantial value, all of which was locked up in real estate, and he had never considered the imminent need for liquidity. Also his business, by nature, faces substantial exposures because of the operation of heavy equipment in his community, but he had ignored all the strategies available to protect his family assets from potential lawsuits.

Multiple problems needed to be solved, but our firm's philosophy is to approach even big problems like this in a step-by-step manner. Clearly, the first step was to initiate a plan for Stuart to realize the full value of the business while supporting the continued growth and success of the company. Once that transition was secure, many of the estate planning needs and goals could fall into place.

The company had one advantage that favored an ESOP—it is an S corporation business. An ESOP can effectively provide a market for the shares of owners looking to retire or as a way to gain access to the current value of the company they have built, providing a benefit and job security for employers in the process. But an S corporation ESOP is even more effective. The trust is federal tax free (state tax is low-to-zero depending on the state), and the trust is the single shareholder. The S corporation is taxed at the shareholder rate, and the S corporation ESOP is a tax fee trust, so provided the sale is for 100 percent of the stock, you now have a tax free business! The company can operate without paying federal income taxes, and those tax savings can fund the transfer of ownership.

The Solution

We established an S corporation ESOP with an installment sale funded by a five-year note from Stuart. The obligation is being paid through the tax savings the company achieves by operating as an S corporation ESOP, so there is no drain on company cash flow, operations, or expansion plans.

The value of the asset is now established by actual sale for estate tax purposes instead of having to use asset-freeze techniques or resorting to an IRS appraisal after Stuart is deceased. Meanwhile, with the installment sale, the gain from the sale is taxed as capital gains, and the family's financial liabilities in connection with the business are now managed but with the ESOP as owner.

To assure his ability to attract and retain the management talent needed for an employee-owned company, we established a nonqualified benefit plan for key employees, informally funded by life insurance. Next, the company purchased a five-year term policy on Stuart to assure payment of the note to his heirs if Stuart was to die prior to the completion of the installment period.

As with all Employee Retirement Income Security Act plans, overlooking any of the myriad details of implementing an ESOP, particularly an S corporation ESOP, puts its tax-qualified status at considerable risk. Yet, when handled by experts with years of practical experience, the tasks can be completed within 60 days, as they were for Stuart Mortensen.

The Result

The business and family pressure that was building over Stuart's exit has been relieved, and the continued success of a multigenerational company is now secured. The business has been removed from the Mortensen estate, so liquidity needed for asset distribution and estate taxes in the future have been achieved.

(continued)

(continued)

Key Questions

Advisers should be asking their clients in similar situations the following questions:

- If it takes five years to plan and execute a business exit strategy, when is the right time for you to start the process that will assure your company's long-term continuity and success?
- If you have an S corporation, are you aware that with a properly drafted S corporation ESOP owning 100 percent of the shares, your company can operate without paying federal income taxes?
- Because your business is the largest asset in your estate, and continued family ownership is not an option, have you considered what your other options could be to capture the maximum value of that asset for your family legacy?

Ellwood L. Jones
Capital Region Financial Group, LLC
Folsom, CA